Hong Kong

at its best

More praise for Robert S. Kane...

"The strength of Kane's books lies in their personal flavor and zestful writing style. He doesn't shy away from expressing opinion, is strong on culture, art, and history, along with dining and shopping."
— Jack Schnedler, *Chicago Sun-Times*

"Kane's books take the reader beyond the expected. His works are carefully researched, succinctly presented and opinionated."
— Jane Abrams, *New York Daily News*

"Kane is a man of perception and taste, with a knowledge of art, architecture and history. He doesn't spare the occasional sharp evaluation if something is less than the highest quality."
— Lois Fegan, *Jersey Journal*

"Anyone going should take one of Bob Kane's books."
— Paul Jackson, *New York Post*

"Kane's candor, conciseness and credibility have made his books among the top selling in the travel field—a must for travelers."
— Joel Sleed, *Newhouse News Service*

"Kane does not mince words. His choices, ranked according to price, service, location and ambience, are selective; he provides opinions."
— Ralph Gardner, *San Antonio Express-News*

"Kane wanders the globe, testing pillows, mattresses and, in some cases, abominable food in order to be a faithful guide, writing his own observations, and leaving nothing to ghost writers or a band of behind-the-scenes reporters; Kane's unafraid to recommmend some places and condemn others."
— Maria Lisella, *The Travel Agent*

Robert S. Kane

Hong Kong
at its best

WITH *MACAU* AND CHINA'S TOP THREE CITIES:
BEIJING, SHANGHAI, GUANGZHOU (CANTON)

Printed on recyclable paper

PASSPORT BOOKS
a division of *NTC Publishing Group*
Lincolnwood, Illinois USA

BY ROBERT S. KANE

The World at Its Best Travel Series
BRITAIN AT ITS BEST
FRANCE AT ITS BEST
GERMANY AT ITS BEST
HAWAII AT ITS BEST
HOLLAND AT ITS BEST
HONG KONG AT ITS BEST
ITALY AT ITS BEST
LONDON AT ITS BEST
NEW YORK AT ITS BEST
PARIS AT ITS BEST
SPAIN AT ITS BEST
SWITZERLAND AT ITS BEST
WASHINGTON, D.C. AT ITS BEST

A to Z World Travel Guides
GRAND TOUR A TO Z: THE CAPITALS OF EUROPE
EASTERN EUROPE A TO Z
SOUTH PACIFIC A TO Z
CANADA A TO Z
ASIA A TO Z
SOUTH AMERICA A TO Z
AFRICA A TO Z

1996 Printing

Published by Passport Books, a division of NTC Publishing Group.
4255 West Touhy Avenue
Lincolnwood (Chicago), Illinois 60646-1975 U.S.A.
© 1992 by Robert S. Kane. All rights reserved. No part of this book may be
reproduced, stored in a retrieval system, or transmitted in any form or by any
means, electronic, mechanical, photocopying, or otherwise, without the prior
written permission of NTC Publishing Group.
Manufactured in the United States of America.
Library of Congress Catalog Card Number: 91-62828

6 7 8 9 ML 9 8 7 6 5 4 3

For William F. Peper

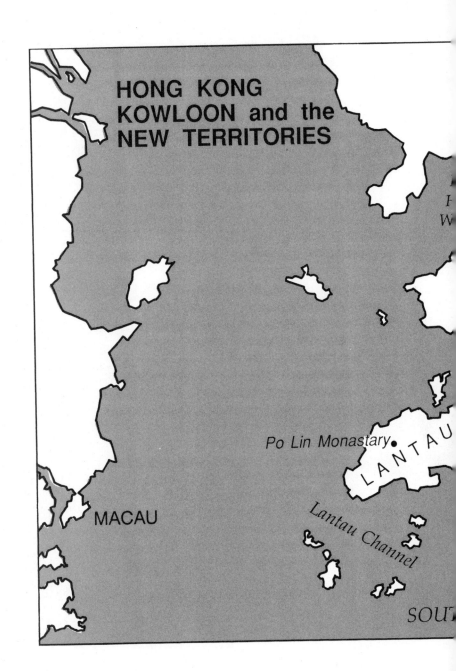

HONG KONG
KOWLOON and the
NEW TERRITORIES

Po Lin Monastery.

LANTAU

MACAU

Lantau Channel

SOUT

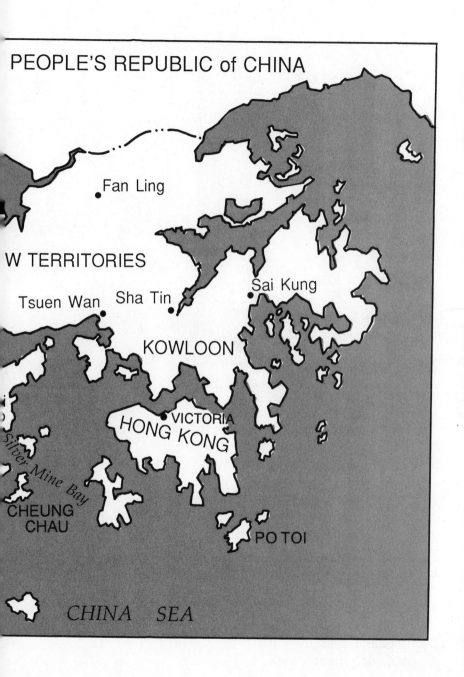

PEOPLE'S REPUBLIC of CHINA

Fan Ling

W TERRITORIES

Tsuen Wan   Sha Tin   Sai Kung

KOWLOON

VICTORIA
HONG KONG

Silver Mine Bay

CHEUNG
CHAU

PO TOI

CHINA SEA

Contents

Foreword

The Dynamism of Hong Kong

Hong Kong evolves in cycles. Since Britain obtained this small-in-area but significant territory from China in the mid-nineteenth century, it has grown economically powerful out of all proportion to its size, the while increasingly attractive to curious travelers making their way through east Asia.

When I first knew it a quarter-century back, you paid Hong Kong a visit—usually in the course of a journey including Japan and Thailand if not also the Philippines—because you knew it would be the closest you would get to the immense People's Republic of China—then off limits to Westerners. Later, on revisits to Hong Kong I found that China had relaxed its isolationist philosophy to the extent that it exported crafts and textiles and jewelry to Hong Kong and it became just the ticket for traveling shoppers who could be the first on their block to take home made-in-Communist China souvenirs.

Before long, a substantial visitor industry developed, and you had still another reason for a Hong Kong holiday: custom-made clothing (men's suits especially, but women's garments, too) at rock-bottom tabs. Later on, China entered the profitable tourism market, and Hong Kong found itself welcoming China visitors either immediately in advance of, or just after China exploration. As recently as a decade back, when visitor facilities on the Mainland were, to understate, unpretentious, you were especially glad of Hong Kong pampering, either pre- or post-China.

Recent seasons have seen Hong Kong develop as a destination of international consequence primarily because outlanders are curious about this small-in-area British colony that has become important enough for Beijing to have negotiated with London for its return to the Chinese fold, just three years before the twentieth century becomes the twenty-first.

This in-between period—Hong Kong's final British years—has been the most fascinating time, for me, at least, to visit the territory. The point of the pages following is to explain why, employing the specifics with which you're familiar if you know any of the dozen additional titles of my *World at Its Best* series.

I open with background, in no global destination more unusual than in this rich territory, with the majority of its nearly six million residents Chinese (and Cantonese-speaking), supplemented by a significant British minority as representatives of the mother country, with a sprinkling of foreigners to add spice. You will update yourself on nitty-gritty at the commencement of this book—business hours in shops and offices through counsel on what to pack and, if you're not already proficient, how to maneuver the chopsticks with which you'll be confronted in every restaurant you enter that specializes in the cuisine of China (rightfully considered one of the three world greats, along with those of France and Italy).

So that you don't enter—and depart—convinced that the sole excuses for a Hong Kong visit are its shops and custom tailors, I make it a point—after brief briefings on matters like history and geography, currency and tipping—to introduce you to cultural Hong Kong—its Philharmonic and concert halls and theaters. Of course there's background on drinks and discos, but Hong Kong is a land of gorgeous festivals (I bring the most spectacular to your attention) and of other diversions, the range golf and horse-racing, snorkeling and sailing, through visits to Chinese temples, underappreciated treasure-filled museums, aged walled villages and little-known offshore islands.

The glory of Hong Kong is that it is, at one and the same time, Chinese and (for the next half decade) British. Even after the central government in Beijing takes command, English is slated to remain a principal language (together with Cantonese), as it is today. And I remain convinced, along with a fairly substantial segment (if not all) of resident Hong Kongers, that the territory's specialties—superb hotels superbly operated (managements are both Chinese and imported, staffs dominantly Chinese), as wide a range of restaurants as you will find in New York and London, not to mention the stores and the tailors—will continue to serve as the backbone of its tourist industry, when it becomes, officially, a Special Administrative Region of the People's Republic of China on July 1, 1997, by terms of the "one country, two systems" Sino-British Joint Declaration signed in 1984—whose terms preserve Hong Kong's legal, fiscal, monetary, social and governmental systems, its free-market economic policies and—hardly unimportant—its cosmopolitan lifestyle.

As the Hong Kong Government has put it succinctly—and well—in a publication: "1997 is not a full stop but a comma." Hong Kong is southern China's principal source of foreign investments, foreign exchange earnings, management expertise and technological skills. Indeed, two thirds of the foreign investment in China derives from Hong Kong, and two million workers within China proper are employees of Hong Kong-based companies.

Hong Kong hotels, and restaurant and shop staffs treat us visitors well because they appreciate that we're valued players in the tourism game—and they know that tourism is the territory's third largest earner of foreign exchange. In chapters following, you'll find evaluations—my own, based on personal sampling—of half a hundred Hong Kong hotels (plus substantial choice of hotels in excursion territory: adjacent Portuguese Macau, and the mainland Chinese cities of Beijing, Guangzhou [Canton] and Shanghai—to which I devote chapters). They're divided into the three categories I employ in all the books of my series—Luxury, First Class, and Moderate, as indeed are some 70 Hong Kong restaurants (not only Chinese, but serving a dozen-plus foreign cuisines) in addition to a solid choice of eateries in Macau and the trio of major Chinese cities.

Close to six million of us visit Hong Kong each year. That figure goes up annually, as indeed does the number of hotel rooms, with the total some 35,000. I like to think I know why: Hong Kong is exotic, luxurious, comfortable, delicious and—not unimportant, this—strategically situated, making possible forays (as brief as a day) into China, not to mention other lands of southeast Asia, Japan to Thailand.

Elsewhere in your travels, you may feel guilty about indulging in posh hotels, dining lavishly, and shopping extravagantly. But not in Hong Kong, where it is the very rare visitor who doesn't have a smashing good time.

ROBERT S. KANE

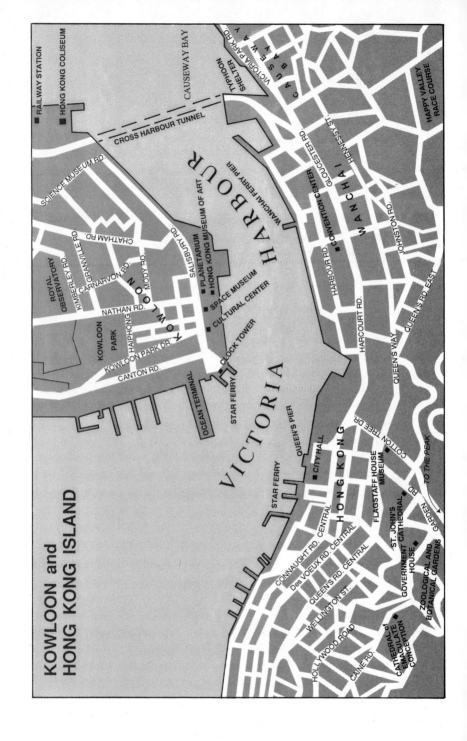

KOWLOON and
HONG KONG ISLAND

■ RAILWAY STATION
■ HONG KONG COLISEUM

CROSS HARBOUR TUNNEL

CAUSEWAY BAY

TYPHOON SHELTER

VICTORIA PARK

CAUSEWAY RD.

HAPPY VALLEY RACE COURSE

WANCHAI FERRY PIER

HONG KONG MUSEUM OF ART
PLANETARIUM
SPACE MUSEUM
CULTURAL CENTER
CLOCK TOWER

SALISBURY RD.

SCIENCE MUSEUM RD.

ROYAL OBSERVATORY

KIMBERLEY RD.
CARNARVON RD.
GRANVILLE RD.
CHATHAM RD.
MODY RD.

NATHAN RD.

KOWLOON PARK

HAIPHONG

KOWLOON PARK DR.

CANTON RD.

KOWLOON

OCEAN TERMINAL

STAR FERRY

HARBOUR

VICTORIA   HARBOUR

WANCHAI

CONVENTION CENTER
GLOUCESTER ST.
HENNESSY ST.

HARBOUR RD.
JOHNSTON RD.

QUEEN'S RD. EAST

HARCOURT RD.

QUEEN'S WAY

COTTON TREE DR.

TO THE PEAK

HONG KONG

QUEEN'S PIER

CITY HALL

STAR FERRY

FLAGSTAFF HOUSE MUSEUM

ST. JOHN'S CATHEDRAL
GOVERNMENT HOUSE
ZOOLOGICAL AND BOTANICAL GARDENS
GARDEN RD.

CONNAUGHT RD. CENTRAL
Des VOEUX RD. CENTRAL
QUEEN'S RD. CENTRAL
WELLINGTON ST.
HOLLYWOOD ROAD
CANE RD.

CATHEDRAL of EMMACULATE CONCEPTION

Hong Kong to Note

ADDRESSES

Hong Kong Tourist Association's offices in the United States are at 590 Fifth Avenue, New York, N.Y. 10036; 333 North Michigan Avenue, Chicago, IL 60601; and 10940 Wilshire Boulevard, Los Angeles, CA 90024. The association's Canadian office is at 347 Bay Street, Toronto, Ontario. European outposts include offices at 125 Pall Mall, London, and 38 Avenue George V, Paris. If you're proceeding to Hong Kong from Japan, it might be worth knowing that HKTA, in that country, is at Toho Twin Tower Building, Yurakucho, Tokyo, and Hong Kong & China Bank Building, Chuo-ku, Osaka. HKTA's information centers on home base in Hong Kong are at Star Ferry Concourse, Kowloon; in the basement of Jardine House, 1 Connaught Place, Central, Hong Kong, and—for arriving visitors only—at Hong Kong International Airport. (The association's head office is on the 35th floor of Jardine House.)

BUSINESS HOURS

Department stores and certain better shops in the classier arcades are open Monday through Saturday, 11 A.M. to 6

P.M.; most other shops are open 10 A.M. to between 9 P.M. and 10 P.M. daily. Many shops are open Sundays. Offices are open from 9 A.M. to 5 P.M., Monday through Friday, and usually closed for lunch between 1 and 2 P.M. on those days. Offices are open on Saturdays 9 A.M. to 1 P.M. Major banks—especially for many Americans who are used to skimpy 9 A.M. to 3 P.M. banking on weekdays only—have super hours: 9 A.M. to 4:30 P.M. weekdays, plus 9 A.M. to 12:30 P.M. Saturdays.

CALENDAR OF EVENTS

January: New Year's Day (public holiday), Hong Kong Arts Festival (into February), Japanese Film Week, opening of Hong Kong Ballet season, horseracing at Happy Valley and Shatin race courses.

February: Hong Kong Ballet and Hong Kong Arts Festival continue, Hong Kong Philharmonic season opens, Hong Kong Golf Open, Hong Kong Chinese Orchestra season opens, Lunar New Year's Days (public holiday—dates vary) with fireworks displays, Hong Kong Ladies Open Amateur Golf Championships.

March: Hong Kong Food Festival, Urban Council Tennis Competition, Hong Kong Chinese Orchestra season opens, Cathay Pacific-Hong Kong Bank International Seven-A-Side Rugby games, Hong Kong International Handball Invitation Tournament, Hong Kong Youth Badminton Competition.

April: Salem Tennis Open, Hong Kong International Film Festival, Ching Ming Festival (public holiday), Hong Kong Annual Badminton Championships.

May: Birthday of Tin Hau (special tours), Buddha's Birthday, Cheung Chau Bun Festival (public holiday), Hong Kong–Macau Interport Matches.

June: Queen's Birthday (public holiday), Dragon Boat Festival (public holiday).

July: Summer Fun Festival, International Arts Carnival, International Dance Festival.

August: Master Photographs Exhibition, Hong Kong Intercity Contract Bridge Championship, Hungry Ghost Festival.

September: South China Athletics Association Championships, British Film Week, Mid-Autumn Lantern Design Competition and Exhibition, Mid-Autumn Festival.

October: Birthday of Confucius, Chung Yeung Festival (public holiday), Asian Regatta, Pacific Bowling Championships.

November: Hong Kong Rowing Championships, Hong Kong Cup, Hong Kong International Kart Grand Prix, Clearwater Bay Open Tennis Championships, Windsurfing Championships.

December: Christmas Carnival, Christmas (public holiday).

CATHAY PACIFIC AIRWAYS

Cathay Pacific—Hong Kong headquartered—links its home base with major Asian points, including Beijing, Bombay, Bangkok, Jakarta, Shanghai, Singapore, and Tokyo, but flies as well to and from Los Angeles; its daily flights are the only nonstops between LA and Hong Kong. (You depart California at 2 P.M. and arrive at 8 P.M. the next day in Hong Kong.) Cathay Pacific works closely with the crack U.S. carrier, American Airlines, which has flights to major U.S. cities that connect with those of Cathay Pacific. So that if, for example, you're on the East Coast or in the Midwest, you may select an American flight which will connect with Cathay Pacific's.

The conception of two aviators—American Roy Farrell and Australian Sydney de Kantzow—following World War II, Cathay Pacific was launched when each of the founders laid out a Hong Kong dollar to register the airline, whose original fleet was not difficult to keep track of: a pair of DC-3s. The carrier started service with charters, primarily between Hong Kong and Australia, and within Southeast Asia, to such points as Bangkok, Macau, and Rangoon, occasionally going as far afield as London and Auckland, in New Zealand.

In 1948, a landmark Cathay Pacific year, 45 percent of its stock was acquired by the Swire Group, now its owners. The early 1950s saw two passenger classes and a more extensive route system, with service to major Pacific points. The fleet turned jet in the 1960s, and in the 1970s, expansion burgeoned, with routes to North America (Vancouver was the first New World destination), and to Europe, initially London and Frankfurt. CP service to Paris was the first nonstop linking Hong Kong and the French capital.

Today, Cathay Pacific—whose alert crews come from ten Asian countries, and with a worldwide staff totaling 6,000—operates the only entirely Rolls-Royce–powered wide-bodied fleet, having pioneered ultralong-haul nonstops between Hong Kong and major European capitals as well as Australia and North America. Its owning company's Swire Air Caterers, jointly operated by the Swire Group and the Hong Kong–based Peninsula Hotels Group, supplies in-flight meals to twenty airlines serving Hong Kong's Kai Tak Airport, with the food so good that Cathay Pacific has been tapped a member of the snooty international group of restaurateurs, Confrérie de la Chaine des Rotisseurs.

CATHEDRALS AND CHURCHES

Hong Kong has a substantial Christian community. There are both Roman Catholic and Protestant cathedrals (Chapter 2) and a number of churches.

CHINA AND MACAU

These are, certainly in my view, requisite destinations for the visitor in Hong Kong. I include chapters on excursions to the three major Chinese cities (Beijing, Guangzhou [Canton], and Shanghai), and to the Portuguese territory of Macau, on later pages.

CHOPSTICKS

In most Chinese restaurants places are set with chopsticks rather than silverware—which must be specially requested. Chopsticks are an ingenious Chinese invention, and you find that your dexterity increases as you use them. Here's how, in three easy steps: 1. Hold one chopstick firmly between the joint of your thumb and the tip of your third finger; 2. Then hold the second chopstick between the tip of your thumb and the tips of your first and second fingers; 3. The lower chopstick remains rigid while you move the upper chopstick in a pincer movement to pick up the food. Tables in Chinese restaurants are set also with a Chinese-style spoon, for soups and other dishes for which chopsticks are not practical, two bowls (one for rice, one for soup), teacup and saucer, and usually a small dish in whose compartments are mustard and chili sauce, as well as a dish of soy sauce.

CLIMATE

Hong Kong is what might be called mild temperate—with four seasons. Winter—the first two or two and a half months of the year—can be as low as the 30s Fahrenheit, which means cold, but can be much warmer, too. Spring and autumn are typically mid-cool/mid-warm, with the fall months through to the year's end the most agreeable, in the 50s and 60s Fahrenheit. The latter season—fall—is often the pleasantest; spring can be cloudy—a kind of prelude to frequently humid, oft-rainy (and upon occasion really stormy) summers when temperatures can ascend to the high 80s, with considerable sunshine to offset the rain—upon occasion of typhoon velocity. My philosophy, with respect to travel to Hong Kong or to anywhere for that matter, is go when you can, dealing with weather as you encounter it.

CLOTHES

Dress more or less as you would at home, casually while sightseeing, dressier in the evening at better restaurants, when men will want jacket and tie. If your visit will be in winter, have warmer clothes. At all seasons, be with raincoat and umbrella.

CREDIT CARDS

Just about everybody accepts them, but when you bargain over a purchase (and bargaining is a popular practice; see SHOPPING below), the merchant will give you a better price for cash, there being no seller's fee to pay to the credit-card company in such an instance. Popular cards include *American Express, Diners Club, MasterCard,* and *Visa.* Increasingly, because American Express and Diners Club fees to participating restaurants, shops, hotels, and the like are higher than what bank cards charge, you find places that accept only bank cards (Visa and/or MasterCard), so do be sure to carry these with you.

CUISINE

You will have had Chinese food in restaurants at home, and you no doubt appreciate even before arrival that it's one of the world's great cuisines (experts rank it in an exalted trio along with French and Italian, where it most certainly belongs). Chinese restaurants in Hong Kong are among the best in the world (better, by and large, than those in China, which lacks the wealth—and, thus, the quality restaurants—of rich, tourist-packed Hong Kong). You'll have the opportunity in Hong Kong to sample the great regional cuisines of China—Szechuan, Beijing (often still termed Peking—the cuisine, if not the city), Shanghai, Hunan, Cantonese, and the least known of the lot—found often in the south—Chiu Chow. Number of dishes to order? The old rule—one per person plus an additional dish—is a good rule. Make a point in Hong Kong of trying seafood—Western-style, of course, but as the basis of countless Chinese dishes, as well, remembering that you are in seafood territory; there are some 24,000 fishermen at work on 5,000 boats, off Hong Kong shores, from which the annual haul is close to 220,000 tons.

And in Hong Kong's Chinese restaurants you select your own seafood; it would be difficult to find an eatery without at least one fish tank or aquarium on the premises. Other good bets for Chinese lunches and dinners? Crispy Peking duck; poached shrimp with ginger and garlic; duck with bean curd, ginger, and scallions; seasonal fish, shrimp, and other seafood, baked pork ribs; braised mushrooms and bamboo shoots; roast chicken in lemon sauce; beggar's chicken; drunken chicken; eight-treasure duck; and superb noodles in a near-endless variety of shapes and textures, including transparent or "cellophane" noodles embellishing soups, meats, and vegetables.

If you're on a business trip, there's a good chance your hosts will tender a banquet in your honor. At restaurant banquets, be prepared for as many as a dozen dishes, starting with a cold course, and ending with soup, noodles or rice, and dessert. Seem like a lot? It does, but mark my words, consuming such a repast is as effortless as the food is delicious; and you help yourself to as much or as little of each course as you like.

It's a good plan—one that I follow—to have one Chinese and one Western meal a day, a system that precludes too much of a good thing. Western restaurants are often at their best in better hotels; you'll find places specializing in steak and French and Italian cuisines. I devote a chapter of this book to Hong Kong's restaurants.

Dim Sum—which translates from the Chinese as "savory snacks," are just that. They constitute the contents of the carts on which they're loaded, and which you see servers in restaurants wheeling around to customers, who select from them. The Chinese eat *dim sum* for breakfast as well as lunch. Westerners tend to skip them as the first meal of the day, but they're delicious for lunch, when an à la carte order of three or four make a fabulous meal. The range is steamed minced pork and shrimp dumplings, steamed chicken roll in bean curd wrapper, and shrimp-filled rice flour rolls through spare ribs with red pepper sauce, dumplings with minced pork, and chicken soup with minced beef balls.

CULTURAL HONG KONG

Hong Kong has become a major Asian cultural center, with its state-of-the-art, multi-hall *Hong Kong Cultural Centre*, home base for the *Hong Kong Philharmonic* (which performs 100 domestic concerts annually, and in other venues as well), the *Hong Kong Academy for Performing Arts* (with its 1,200-seat Lyric Theater, concert hall, recital hall, and studio theater), *Hong Kong Arts Centre* (for movies, art shows, and lectures as well as performances in its Shouson Theater), and the *City Hall's* concert hall and theater.

CURRENCY

Americans, Canadians, and citizens of other countries where the unit of currency is called the dollar: take note.

You're in still another dollar country. The Hong Kong dollar is written "HK$____," with notes in denominations of HK$10, HK$20, HK$50, HK$100, HK$500, and HK$1,000, with 10¢, 20¢, 50¢, HK$1, HK$2, HK$5 denominations in coins. For easily a decade, the rate of exchange has been approximately HK$8 to one U.S. dollar. As in most countries, you receive better rates when you change your money in the banks rather than at hotels. There are currency exchange firms, as well.

CUSTOMS AND VISAS

You may take in to Hong Kong a quart of liquor, 200 cigarettes, 50 cigars, or a half-pound of tobacco, as well as cologne and perfume in reasonable amounts. Visas are not necessary for Americans who stay no longer than thirty days. Canadian citizens, coming from a British Commonwealth country, as is Hong Kong, may stay ninety days without a visa. If you know your stay will be longer than either of these periods, apply for a visa before departure for Hong Kong at the British Embassy in Washington, the British High Commission in Ottawa, or any British consulate-general or consulate.

Returning to the United States: Each individual may bring back $400 worth of purchases duty free. That is allowable once every thirty days, provided you've been out of the country at least forty-eight hours. If you've spent more than $400 you may be charged a flat 10 percent duty on the next $1,000 worth of purchases. Remember, too, that antiques, duly certified to be at least 100 years old, are admitted duty-free and do not count as part of your $400 quota; neither do paintings, sculptures, and other works of art, of any date, if certified as original; it's advisable that certification, from the seller or other authority, as to their authenticity, accompany them. Also exempt from duty, but as part of the $400 quota: one quart of liquor. And—this is important—there is no restriction on how much one brings in beyond the $400 limit, so long as the duty is paid.

DRINKS AND DISCOS

Hong Kong is, to put it in a single word, permissive. You may drink in British-style pubs (and, yes, play British-style darts); more conventional bars (many feature early-evening happy hours when tabs are lower); hotel cocktail lounges; restaurants; both Western- and Chinese-style nightclubs, the latter more casual, many of both types with dancing and some with entertainment; and hostess clubs—distinctively Hong Kong institutions, where beverages are consumed in the company of young ladies, invariably attractive, in the employ of the establishment—*and* of the visitor who pays for their drinks, and often—including later on—for their time as well, on a quarter-hourly basis. Some of these spots have so-called VIP rooms for which there is a charge, as well as other extras. In all events, ask for names of and background on currently trendy spots from your hotel concierge—so you have an idea of what you're getting into, and of what it might cost. Western-style late-hours discos, sans hostesses? But of course. They can be pretty fancy, and jammed on weekends, when entrance fees are steeper than weeknights, albeit usually with a drink or two included.

ELECTRIC CURRENT

200 volts, 50 cycles. Your hotel will give you an adapter for your hair dryer or other appliances.

FESTIVALS

Lunar (or, to us, Chinese) *New Year* occupies several late January or early February days, inconvenient for many visitors because most shops—and certain other places as well—are closed. This is a holiday to avoid, if you possibly can, although its final day, *Yuen Siu*, is colorful, with lanterns lighting up parks and gardens, and special festivities. The spring *Dragon Boat Festival* is the time of Hong Kong's traditional boat races. *Tin Hau* honors the goddess of the sea, whose name it takes, with fishing vessels especially decorated, parades, and folk dances. *Mid-Autumn Festival* (the fall day on which it occurs varies) sees people eating strange pastries called moon cakes, with lanterns everywhere after dark. *Winter Solstice* (late December) sees many shops closed, and like Lunar New Year, is not a happy time for visitors—except that it occupies only a single day. The *Hong Kong Asian Arts Festival* is a biennial autumn event, featuring music, theater, and dance from throughout the Far East. The *Hong Kong Arts Festival* traditionally takes place over a three-week winter period, with performing artists and arts groups imported from all over the world. And finally, the *Hong Kong Food Festival* highlights each spring, with market visits, cooking classes, culinary tours, lunch and dinner cruises, and special exhibitions.

GEOGRAPHY IN A NUTSHELL

Look at a map of Asia to see how really small Hong Kong is in area, compared to giant China proper, at whose southeastern tip it is located, bordering the Chinese province of Guangdong, on an estuary of the Pearl River, only 90 miles south of Guangzhou (Canton) and but 40 miles to the east of Macau. Total area is just under 400 square miles (the tiny American state of Rhode Island is more than twice as large) and that includes 235 outlying islands, together with the *New Territories* (366 square miles) and *Kowloon* (4 square miles) on the mainland, as well as *Hong Kong Island* (29 square miles, and often called simply Hong Kong by the locals), across that part of the South China Sea called Victoria Harbour.

GOLF

Avid golfers would work in nine holes atop Everest if they could. Hong Kong is easier. There are a number of golf courses and clubs and unless you can work out entry to one of them through your home club, join the Hong Kong Tourist Association's Sports and Recreation Tour, which includes admission to and lunch at *Clearwater Bay Golf and Country Club*—with greens fees extra, per eighteen holes. The *Discovery Bay* course on Lantau Island stands out because of the views it affords from its mountaintop location. Clubs have pro shops and the Japanese department stores in Causeway Bay (Chapter 5) are good sources of equipment.

GOVERNMENT

Hong Kong, to use the official terminology, at least as Britain uses it, is a British Crown Colony, with an appointed governor and Elizabeth II its queen. Locally, however, recent years have seen it termed a British Administered Territory, and in the press and in speech, simply as "the territory." When Hong Kong becomes a part of China in 1997—ending 150 years of British rule—it will be officially designated as the *Hong Kong Special Administrative Region of the People's Republic of China.*

Surprisingly enough, to Western visitors at least, the territory has not, until very recently, enjoyed as much self-government as one would have expected in the British Commonwealth. Only in 1990 did the Hong Kong Government provide for direct election of legislators, the idea being, reportedly, to establish a strong democracy within the territory before relinquishing control to China. The process began—many Hong Kong residents called it a case of too little too late—with the election of eighteen of the sixty members of the Legislative Council in 1991. Heretofore, Legislative Council members were appointed by the colonial government or, in some cases, indirectly elected by constituency groups divided by profession—teachers, lawyers, business executives, and the like. Only lower-down district level officials had been popularly elected. Unlike in the Mother Country, where the minimum voting age is 18, Hong Kong's is 21.

The years ahead? According to the 1984 agreement between Britain and China—popularly referred to in Hong Kong as the "Joint Declaration"—Hong Kong will remain capitalist, while China proper continues Communist. The declaration states that Hong Kong will be allowed to govern itself domestically and retain its own currency for a minimum period of half a century, with China responsible for its defense and foreign affairs. Although there has been considerable recent immigration from Hong Kong to foreign parts, Hong Kong people have increased contacts with the Chinese province—Guangdong—just across the frontier. Hong Kong residents cross over to shop, and Hong Kong factories have taken over counterparts in China, where wages are lower.

The future? Every Hong Kong resident you speak to has his or her own opinion. Some are pessimistic as to whether China will adhere scrupulously to terms of the agreement; others believe China appreciates that a capitalist, self-governing Hong Kong with a strong and wealthy economy cannot but benefit China. The effect of all this for the visitor in today's Hong Kong? So far as my experience indicates, it's operating as brilliantly as ever—which is going some.

HISTORY CAPSULIZED

For long a part of China politically as well as geographically, Hong Kong—a free port (alas with alcohol, perfume, and tobacco taxed) considered to be the third largest financial center in the world—was first occupied by the British during the Opium War in 1839. London knew it had a valuable, strategically situated colony, which prospered as the commercial gateway to southern China, while becoming respected throughout Asia for its British-operated banks, shipping companies, and other international enterprises. As the nineteenth century became the twentieth, Hong Kong continued to develop.

But just eighteen days after the Japanese, on December 7, 1941, bombed America's Pearl Harbor in Hawaii (bringing the U.S. into World War II), the Japanese conquered Hong Kong, retaining it through the war, after which—in 1945—it again flew the British flag. Starting in 1949, refugees from Communist-controlled China began to swell Hong Kong's ranks. It became one of the most densely populated areas of the planet, to the point where—before the government could build new housing and schools and provide social services for the refugees—overcrowding presented problems of considerable magnitude well into the 1950s. The late 1960s saw strikes and riots—a consequence of China's Cultural Revolution—spill over the border into Hong Kong. Within a decade, relations were better between enormous China and the tiny colony. The former began to appreciate that the latter was a significant source of foreign exchange and an important opening to what was then, to China, still a fairly remote outside world.

Hong Kong today is universally respected for commercial savoir faire, and its strategic situation, at the edge of China, is a location instrumental in luring to it close to six million visitors each year. In 1997, change "the edge of China" to "within" China; at that time the rich little British colony is to be politically reattached to the country of which it had long been a part.

HORSERACING

Racing is exceptionally popular, more so than in many places. There are two tracks—*Happy Valley* (Hong Kong Island) and *Shatin* (New Territories). Each is ultramod, with the latest equipment and giant color display screens facing stands, so you don't lose track of the horses. Racing is the only form of legal gambling, the Hong Kong Lottery excepted, and each of the racetracks is big—with a capacity of nearly 49,000. Races take place Wednesday evenings and weekends (Saturday or Sunday), June into September, and the Hong Kong Tourist Association runs well-organized racing tours to both courses (select your preference), which include admission, a meal, and transportation. To bet, you must be at least 18. Watch the daily newspapers for detailed results.

LANGUAGES AND POPULATION

All but two percent of Hong Kong's 5.8 million residents are ethnic Chinese, and mostly Cantonese at that. Not surprisingly, Cantonese is the principal official language, with English the second official language. It is spoken at hotel desks and in better restaurants and shops. But, despite the fact that (at least until 1997) Hong Kong is a British territory, you must *not* expect to find English spoken universally. By no means.

LOCAL LITERATURE

There are two good daily English-language newspapers: the *South China Morning Post*—better known abroad of the pair—and the *Hong Kong Standard*. Hong Kong Tourist Association publishes a *Weekly Calendar of Events;* free from its offices (addresses above).

PASSPORTS

Passports are necessary for admission to Hong Kong (as well, of course, to China and Macau—Chapters 6 through

10—to which you may make excursions from Hong Kong) and must be presented to U.S. Immigration upon your return. Apply at U.S. Department of State passport offices in major cities (look under U.S. Government in the telephone directory) or—in smaller towns—at the office of the clerk of a federal court and, as long as the practice obtains, at certain post offices. Allow four weeks, especially for a first passport (valid for ten years), for which you'll need a pair of two-inch-square photos and a birth certificate or other proof of citizenship. There's a $65 fee (subject to change) for new or renewal adult passports valid for ten years, and $40 for children's (under 18) passports. If you're in a hurry when you apply, say so; Uncle Sam will usually try to expedite if you're able to produce your air or ship ticket or certification from your travel agent that such tickets are reserved. Upon receipt of this valuable document, sign your name where indicated, fill in the address of next of kin, and keep it with you—*not packed in a suitcase*—as you travel. In case of loss, contact local police, the nearest United States Consulate General (or in China, the U.S. Embassy in Beijing) or Passport Office, Department of State, Washington, DC 10524.

SHOPPING

No other Asian destination is as visited for its shops as Hong Kong. I devote substantial detail—all of Chapter 5—to shops, dividing them into two dozen categories.

SPORTS

In addition to golf (above), Hong Kong excels at water sports (swimming, with changing rooms, showers, and cafés at a number of beaches; water-skiing, snorkeling, windsurfing, and sailing). And there are fine facilities, as well, for squash and badminton, tennis and soccer, jogging and climbing, basketball and football, volleyball and handball.

TELEVISION

Watch the papers for programs; Hong Kong has a number of English-language stations, and TV in hotel rooms is standard.

TIPPING

Not a problem. A 10 percent service charge is added to restaurant and hotel bills, and you may, in the case of a restaurant tab, leave a small additional amount, but only if service has been exemplary. Tip taxi drivers minimally, simply by upping the amount to the nearest dollar. And tip doormen and bellmen, albeit not heavily.

TOURS, TOUR OPERATORS, TRAVEL AGENTS

Agents, first: select one who is affiliated with the American Society of Travel Agents (ASTA) and, preferably, who knows Hong Kong—and ideally, China and Macau—first-hand. For an initial trip, some travelers are happy with the convenience of a package. Operators who make a specialty of that part of the world—whose packages may be purchased through retail travel agents—include *Pacific Select, Pacific Delight, Japan & Orient Tours, T. B. I. Tours,* and *United Vacations.*

TRANSPORTATION

Ferries—especially the legendary Star Ferry linking Hong Kong Island and Kowloon on the mainland—are surely the most romantic means of transport. They run between 6:30 A.M. and 11:30 P.M., and the crossing takes but eight minutes. Don't leave Hong Kong without having made at least one Star Ferry crossing. There are additional ferries to Lantau and other islands; they use the Outlying District Ferry Pier on Hong Kong Island.

But you may also cross between Hong Kong and Kowloon via tunnel (in a taxi or rented car). *Taxis* are red on Hong Kong Island and in Kowloon, green in the New Territories, and blue on Lantau Island. Ideally, have your destination *written in Chinese* for the driver, who is paid the fare on the meter, plus a small tip—what's remaining to the nearest dollar. If a taxi takes you through the Cross-Harbour Tunnel, expect the driver to charge you for his return to the other side. *Maxicabs*—yellow with a green stripe—are fixed-price, on specific routes, with a roof sign indicating the final destination. *Buses* are fabulous London-style double-deckers. As at home (at least where I live), *exact change* is required for fare, and you pay according to the distance you're traveling. With yellow-and-red *Minibuses*, advise the driver where you want to get off—anywhere you designate except at a regular bus stop; pay as you alight. *Rickshaws* are virtually extinct—but not quite; agree on the price before setting off. Of course you may rent *cars*—by and large chauffeur-driven rather than self-driven, in Hong Kong. The *MTR (Mass Transit Railway—* what we would call subway) is the fastest means of transport (with air-conditioned cars, and entrance via coin machines). *Trains* ply between Hong Kong and China (travelers to China need a Chinese visa affixed to their passports); the railway station is at Hunghom in Kowloon. And best for last: Hong Kong's absolutely-not-to-be-missed public transport is the *tram* to and from the Peak (Chapter 2).

2

Hong Kong to See

LAY OF THE LAND

If there is a key Hong Kong adjective, it's *deceptive*; deceptively large (more than 400 square miles in area, with a population nearing six million, deceptively appearing as but a dot on the map of Asia, edging the southeast corner of massive China—nothing less than the world's most populous country; deceptively Chinese as regards culture, language, and populace, despite official designation as a British Crown Colony (or, to use the contemporary designation preferred by locals, British Administered Territory), with resident Brits relatively few and far between; deceptively Chinese-speaking (despite English's designation as an official language); deceptive in that its rural precincts—still dotted with aged temples and traditional villages—occupy most of its land area; and deceptive, too, in that even though it is commonly considered as a combination of the island whose name it takes and a stretch of the Chinese mainland, it includes, as well, a veritable network (235 all told) of little-known islands, the largest of which is twice the area of Hong Kong Island.

Hong Kong lies at the mouth of a river variously known as the Canton or the Pearl, just 90 miles south of

Guangzhou (Canton), one of China's great cities, and with a largely Cantonese-speaking population. (Locals involved with foreign visitors, in hotels, shops, better restaurants, transport terminals, and the like, are invariably bilingual, or at least fairly fluent in English.)

For the overwhelming majority of visitors, Hong Kong is most easily seen in thirds: New Territories, its northernmost area, sharing a frontier with the People's Republic of China; Kowloon, the most populous and touristically significant of the mainland areas, due south of New Territories (with its central area also know as Tsimshatsui); and—just across the waters of Hong Kong Harbour to the south, via Star Ferry, a ride on which is in itself a visitor attraction of no little consequence—Hong Kong Island, with its core—formerly called on my early visits, Victoria—but in recent years known simply as either "Hong Kong"—the name of the entire island, or more precisely, Central. Central is the downtown commercial district, which is not actually central, but rather to the west, with the adjacent area called Wanchai more to the center, and the region called Causeway Bay to its east, just beneath Hong Kong's most spectacular natural landmark, the easily ascendable mountain known as the Peak (below).

Central surrounds a clutch of piers—Star Ferry to Kowloon, others to other points—with Central Bus Terminal, City Hall, General Post Office, and an important naval station officially dubbed HMS (Her Majesty's Ship) Tamar (although it's not a vessel), north of a major thoroughfare, Connaught Road, which lies parallel to still another principal street, Des Voeux Road, and its extension to the east, Chater Road. Hollywood Road is lined with antiques and curio shops. Memorably named Ice House Street (which becomes Wyndham Street) and D'Aigular Street are principal north-south thoroughfares, while it's Harcourt Street (later called Gloucester Street) that leads east-west from Central into Wanchai and Causeway Bay. Happy Valley, one of the two racetracks, adjoins the football stadium in Causeway Bay.

If Hong Kong's Central area is distinctly urban—you could be in any big city when you're near the intersection of, say, Ice House Street and Chater Road, with the traffic heavy, the canyonlike roads fringed by sleek high rises, the populace in the same kind of noisy hurry as urban populaces are in New York and Rome—the ambience of Kowloon, just across the harbor, is something else again. It is not, needless to say, bucolic, but despite the presence of a massive clutch of hotels, busy restaurants, and tempting, customer-filled shops, Kowloon is, withal, less frenetic, easier to negotiate, more relaxing.

And, although Kowloon is the area with the majority of hotels, its geography is such that it's easier to negotiate than Hong Kong. Main street—the thoroughfare around which downtown Kowloon was built over the years—is north-south Nathan Road, which cuts through the area, from southerly east-west Salisbury Road. Canton Road is the area's principal north-south artery at its western side, while Chatham Road is a kind of eastern north-south counterpart. Kowloon's Railway Station is at the far eastern edge of Salisbury Road, while at the far western edge of the area is *Kowloon Park*, containing among other landmarks the Hong Kong Museum of History. Kowloon's western frontier is the harbor, with its standout points, going south to north, Star Ferry Terminal, Ocean Terminal, Ocean Centre and Harbour City.

HONG KONG ISLAND

Victoria Peak represents Hong Kong at its most glorious. Aside from seeing to it that Hong Kong is a strategically placed, not to say attractive island, nature endowed it with this mountain—called simply *The* Peak—and with a thousand-foot elevation.

Ascent, by means of the aptly titled Peak Tram, is half the fun. You're transported for less than an American dollar's fare, from the core of Hong Kong, through the clusters of apartment houses somewhat elevated from downtown, beyond a thicket of trees to the panorama of the Kowloon Peninsula and Victoria Harbour directly below, with Peak Station fifth and highest of the stops along the track and the ultimate destination.

Relatively new as Hong Kong history goes, the tram—or at least its predecessors—go back only to 1888, with the first modern road—allowing for car travel (there are buses and of course taxis)—opened in 1924. Before that you hiked up or, if you were upper class, you ascended by means of a sedan chair transported by a quartet of bearers up Old Peak Road. The first tram, team driven, was supplanted in the mid-twenties by an electric system. In 1989, Peak Tramways overhauled and updated, with a Swiss-type funicular.

With its on-high situation (views to both south and north are fabulous), unique in Hong Kong, The Peak has known periods of ugly exclusivity, with houses in its precinct unavailable to non-Brits, and when even English servants had to have the colonial governor's written permission to make an ascent in the line of duty. Before the era of the tram and the highway, the only means of gaining the upper reaches—aside from shoeleather—was sedan chair.

The snob value of The Peak as a place to live extends to early Hong Kong settlement. With the opening of the 1924 road, Hong Kong social climbers set their sights on a Peak home, and it was not until after World War II that the Hong Kong governor's permission was no longer required for Peak residence. Even today, a house on The Peak is the epitome of Hong Kong living and still by no means easy to come by. Withal, some three million travelers ascend annually for extraordinary vistas of the city and the harbor and, in some instances, to undertake walks around the summit.

(Time to ascend by foot from town is about an hour, and there are countless hikes of varying length that can be undertaken once arrived at the summit, which Peak authorities have graded—for your convenience: 1. Difficult; 2. Moderate; and 3. Easy.)

You may explore Lugard or Harlech roads (they're not hilly, I promise) or ascend to the very summit of the mountain via Mount Austin Road. And plan your trip to include midday so that you may have lunch (Chapter 4), perhaps at the restaurant operated by the Peninsula Hotel in town—or at least a midmorning or afternoon snack.

It's half a century since Hong Kong governors spent summers in official digs atop The Peak; their residence has long since been razed, but pretty gardens that framed the house remain—and with benches, so that you may pause in the day's occupation.

Legislative Council (between Statue Square and Chater Garden): I didn't have to read the sign as I passed by. I knew from the look of this colonnaded, pedimented, official-looking structure that it was the colonial legislature. In I went, to learn how correct I had been: The debate I watched from the visitors' gallery was hot and heavy— the subject was local murders—and held me longer than I thought I would stay. By all means hope that the council is in session when you make your visit. The building went up in the last century during the governorship, according to the cornerstone, of Sir Henry Blake. Because you're in a two-language country, members may speak in either Chinese or English; everyone has earphones to hear one language simultaneously translated into the other.

Hong Kong and Shanghai Bank (Chater Garden)— relatively recent, quite splendid, and reputedly the most expensive building in the world, dates to 1985, and is one of a cluster of downtown Hong Kong skyscrapers that are among the most striking in Asia. Take an elevator up to the summit if you like. And do not fail to observe the profiles of other high rises, particularly that of the Bank of China—you'll remember its X-design façade. It was designed by the Chinese-origin American architect, I. M. Pei and is the tallest building in town.

St. John's Cathedral (Garden Road), went up in 1849 as the seat of the Anglican Bishop of Hong Kong, though its style is based on early Gothic. It was lengthened in 1873, and during World War II it was subjected to debasement by occupying Japanese, who used it as a social club. By that time, some of the cathedral's fittings had been hidden away, but no one thought to replace the late-nineteenth-century William Morris–designed stained glass windows, none of which made it through the war, after which the cathedral was treated to a much-needed restoration. Make note of the pews (still original), the nineteenth-century stone font, with the pulpit from the same period, bishop's throne and choir stalls, a half dozen charming chapels, and handsome, garden-flanked exterior.

Cathedral of the Immaculate Conception (Caine Road)—seat of Hong Kong's Roman Catholic bishop—is, like its Anglican counterpart, Gothic, and opened in 1888, ever since which visitors have enthused over its proportions, with the nave well over 180 feet long and more than 50 feet wide, and the transept 90 feet wide. To understate: impressive.

Zoo and Botanical Gardens (Upper Albert Road) are neighbors, with the gardens going back to the 1860s. The zoo, though, is a veritable youngster from the 1970s, with some fabulous birds its most noted residents. You want to pay a visit.

Government House (Upper Albert Road) has been home to Hong Kong's governors since it was completed in the middle of the last century (with some additions and changes by occupying Japanese during World War II). In the early days, there may have been public visiting hours, but there certainly aren't now. Still, it's worth peeking at, as you pass by, and, big deal, the Guv opens the gardens to visitors one spring Sunday per annum.

Hong Kong Park, the territory's largest such, is recent (it had been called Victoria Barracks) with every appurtenance a park should have: fountains and waterfalls, lakes and greenhouses, and as a special kicker, an *Aviary,* with birds from Melanesia.

Man Mo Temple (Ladder Street) is, if nothing else, memorably named. But it has other attributes, including a fairly substantial history. It dates to the 1840s, when Hong Kong Island was ceded to Britain by China. Both Man and Mo, incidentally, are gods, the former of literature and the latter of war. (Ladder Street, the location, is named for its ladderlike incline, so steep that centuries back rich Hong Kongers were carried to its summit in sedan chairs.)

Bonham Strand is not your ordinary Hong Kong street. Over long years its shops have come to house dealers in—are you ready?—snakes, considered locally as just the thing to cure a cold. It's not difficult, in Hong Kong restaurants, to find snake soup on menus.

Hong Kong Convention and Exhibition Center is the pride of Wanchai, the central sector of Hong Kong Island. It houses a pair of enormous exhibit halls, convention hall, two theaters, a couple of dozen meeting rooms, and worry not, sufficient sources of nourishment to keep you going through daylong meetings. Even if you've no business at the center, pay a call if only to ride the escalator to the seventh floor: the view of Hong Kong is from the world's largest glass-curtain wall. Wow!

Victoria Park (Causeway Bay): Have a look early morning, and you'll see what traditional Chinese shadowboxing is all about. Recreational facilities here are noteworthy—tennis courts and swimming pools among them.

Tiger Balm Gardens (a.k.a. in recent years *Aw Boon Haw Gardens*) are the legacy of a local industrialist, which, it might be said, exemplify money more than taste. They constitute hardly distinguished paintings of local legends in a graceless rocky setting. Skippable.

Middle Kingdom (Ocean Park) is an unabashedly commercial and notably successful contemporary complex that portrays shrines and temples, public squares and street scenes, pagodas and palaces of a dozen-plus Chinese dynasties. Besides the authentically reproduced structures themselves, you're put in the spirit by demonstrations of costumed artisans, wine makers, stone carvers, woodblock printers, dancers, and acrobats. Admission is somewhat steep, but costumed guides—English- and Chinese-speaking—are good, and there are shops and a smart restaurant with dishes from almost every gastronomically important region of China. Fun.

Mosque (Nathan Road): Kowloon has a substantial Moslem population, and its big white mosque—with four massive minarets—is put to frequent use. It's open to visitors, but only after advance booking: the tourist office can help with details.

Ladder Street is but one of a number of ladderlike thoroughfares. This one actually takes the name—and with good reason. It's a veritable staircase and a climb up—the ascent exceeds 200 feet—is, as the French might say of such a workout, *bonne pour la ligne*, good for the figure. Location is between Caine and Hollywood roads.

Repulse Bay is the site of Hong Kong's busiest beach, and of what had been the perfectly lovely Repulse Bay Hotel, the territory's No. 1 out-of-town hostelry. Then came developers who tore down the upper stories of the hotel and replaced them with a garish apartment house. The good news is that the lower, Colonial-style portion of the hotel remains as the base of the apartment house, with several eminently worth-visiting restaurants operated by the Peninsula Hotel in town (Chapter 4).

Stanley Market, in the fishing village of Stanley on a pretty southeast peninsula, is a notable source of good buys in both men's and women's clothing and accessories—some of it of excellent quality. A don't miss.

Tin Hau Temple, just outside of Stanley in a village called Ma Hang, is eighteenth-century and locally revered with good reason: A World War II bomb landed in front of the temple—while its interior was packed with local residents—and, miraculously, did not explode. Stanley, not surprisingly, has not forgotten. Note, too, that *Stanley Beach*, fronting a pleasant bay, can be convenient for a swim; it's quite central.

Aberdeen, for as long as I can remember on visits to Hong Kong, the prototypical photogenic village, has become disagreeably contemporary, fraught with high-rise apartments and factories. You may, however, still visit its lively harbor (a not-so-small floating village of locals live aboard their boats), and its mid-nineteenth-century temple.

Swimming and Sunning: You've a choice of beaches, well equipped with changing rooms, showers, snack bars, and lifeguards. In summer, plan your schedule so as to go on a weekday when crowds are smaller. *Repulse Bay* is no doubt the best known of the beaches but *Deep Water Bay* is worth knowing about—easy to reach by taxi from town.

Skyscrapers: Hong Kong Island's Central district's skyline has become a world-class dazzler. Standouts include the People's Republic of China's principal Hong Kong outpost of the *Bank of China* (with offices of nonbank Chinese government departments, as well), the architect—ironically—American (albeit Chinese-origin) I. M. Pei, and the look irregularly delineated. Pei's building is a next-door neighbor of the squat—and older—original Bank of China headquarters. His tower, slim, elegant and almost cathedral-like, with a glass facade punctuated by steel girders creating a network of dramatic diamonds, is, at seventy stories, the highest of high rises worldwide—the U.S.A. excepted. Close by is still another modern masterwork—Norman Foster's unconventionally facaded *Hong Kong and Shanghai Bank,* whose nearly fifty stories are interrupted at eight-story intervals by triangular girders, with ladderlike appurtenances—a pair on each side of the building— providing additional interest. You'll notice still other fine contemporary work—the silvery twin towers of the *Bond Center,* the *Prince of Wales Building,* named for Prince Charles, who dedicated it, and with Army and Navy headquarters offices; the stylish *Landmark Building,* housing one of Hong Kong's poshest collections of shops (about which I write in Chapter 5); tall and substantial *Jardine House* (a bow here to the Hong Kong Tourist Association, whose head office is within it) with distinctive circular windows and more than half a hundred stories; the *Supreme Court,* whose tower contains several dozen courtrooms; and *Exchange Square,* which is not a square but rather a high rise that is home to the globally significant *Hong Kong Stock Exchange*.

University of Hong Kong (Sai Ying Poon, Hong Kong) is one of the territory's two universities. At the other, the *Chinese University of Hong Kong*, Chinese is the language of instruction. At UHK, classes are conducted in English in a multicollege institution on a traditional-style campus, dominated by the multitower, modified Georgian-style *Main Building*, whose central tower is a campus landmark. There are more contemporary structures, some clean-lined, some with Chinese lines, like *Robert Black College*, a relatively recent dorm. I write about both the UHK's and the CUHK's outstanding *museums* on other pages.

Causeway Bay, easternmost of the three principal districts of Hong Kong Central, is perhaps best known to visitors—especially Japanese visitors—as the site of a cluster of Japanese department stores, along with considerable other mercantile activity in lower-priced shops, including factory outlets. It's fun to amble about for an evening. This is the site, as well, of good-sized *Victoria Park*, whose facilities include a pair each of swimming pools and tennis courts; of not-far-distant *Food Street*, so called because of a maze of restaurants, with foreign cuisines as well as Chinese; *Typhoon Shelter*, positively packed with junks when stormy weather is predicted, and at all times vibrant with families who live on permanently moored houseboats; *Tiger Balm* (a.k.a. *Aw Boom Haw*) *Gardens*, about which I write on another page; and last but hardly least, especially if you're a Noel Coward fan, Causeway Bay's *Noon Day Gun*, originally installed by the pioneer mercantile house of Jardine, still fired every day at midday, and seized upon by Noel Coward when he included it in the lyrics of the song, "Mad Dogs and Englishmen."

Wanchai is the quarter of Hong Kong Island immediately to the east of Central district, most absorbing in its market and in the colorful, shop-lined streets thereabouts. *Wanchai Market* (Queen's Road) is at its perkiest in the morning. You might want to combine a visit to it with an inspection of atmospheric, mid-nineteenth-century *Hung Shing Temple* (Hung Shing Road).

KOWLOON

Kowloon is, in essence, the Visitors' Hong Kong—with the majority of hotels (and in all categories, Chapter 3), many restaurants (Chapter 4), and a central location, edging the South China Sea, south of Guangzhou (Canton) on the Chinese mainland and Hong Kong's New Territories, due east of Macau and north of the island of Hong Kong. Aside from exploring (and I wager, making a few purchases in) myriad shops, you'll find other Kowloon diversion.

When I first knew it, Kowloon was called simply Kowloon. Recent seasons have seen its western sector dubbed Tsimshatsui (sounds a bit more Chinese) and adjacent to the east, Tsimshatsui East. A rose by any other name: Kowloon (to this writer at least) the area remains.

Main Street—and a very busy Main Street it is—goes by the name of Nathan Road, running north-south more or less in Kowloon's center, with northerly Austin Road at one extreme and southerly Salisbury Road at the other—this last considerably better known to visitors because it parallels the harbor and is the site not only of the legendary Peninsula Hotel but also of many other hotels and of the much newer and hardly insignificant *Hong Kong Space Museum and Hong Kong Cultural Centre,* as well as piers, including the one that takes you, via Star Ferry, on an eight-minute crossing to Hong Kong Island, with its urban core the commercial and business center of the territory. (Hong Kong, it is important to point out, has two "downtowns"—both big and busy, one each in Kowloon and on Hong Kong Island.)

Bird Market (Hong Lok Street): The Chinese are partial to birds as pets, and I wager you'll not have seen a bird market like this one before. It's wonderful, given their pampering, that the birds keep their svelte figures.

Clock Tower (adjacent to Star Ferry Terminal) is Kowloon's principal landmark: a 135-foot structure that had been attached to the no longer standing Canton-Kowloon train station, now in the quarter called Hunghom.

Harbour City (Canton Road) is a massive mix of shopping malls, the roster including *Ocean Centre, Ocean Galleries,* and *Ocean Terminal,* with *Silvercord Shopping Centre* across a pedestrian bridge, and nearby, *China Hong City* shopping mall, popular with passengers from cruise ships that tie up at Ocean Terminal.

Hunghom —my favorite Hong Kong place-name—is home to the *Hong Kong Coliseum,* a 12,500-seat center for concerts, sports competitions, and exhibits. In the area, too, are factory outlets for Hong Kong made-for-export fashions, men's as well as women's, *Hong Kong Polytechnic Institute* and the *Railway Station,* terminus for trains to and from China.

Temple Street (see also Hong Kong to Buy, Chapter 5) is a busy night market (from 6 P.M., but at its liveliest a few hours thereafter), worth mentioning also at this point because of al fresco theater on its pavements each evening, with an amusing range of palmists and soothsayers, vendors and ambulatory merchants, and, if you hit a good night, clusters of singers adding to the merriment.

Sung Dynasty Village (at the intersection of Mei Lai and Lai Wan roads) is—or at least should be—a requisite destination. It is a surprise-packed authentic re-creation of a village as it might have been during the dynasty whose name it takes—between the tenth and thirteenth centuries. Virtually no aspect of village life seems to have been omitted from the scene: authentically costumed staff, attention to architectural detail, opportunities to look over artifacts we associate with the China of yore: delicately decorated umbrellas and finely painted fans, candles and incense; with a number of spots for traditional refreshments. The village is fun.

Lei Yue Mun Promontory, taking the name of an adjacent village, is of interest to visitors of a certain age; it's from where the Japanese army launched its invasion of Hong Kong in December 1941—the same month the American territory (now state) of Hawaii was bombed by the Japanese, bringing the United States into World War II.

Kowloon Park (with Canton Road to its east and Austin Road to its north) opened a host of recreational facilities as the eighties became the nineties. Most noteworthy are an Olympic-size swimming pool and a well-equipped games room. But this is a lovely park simply for strolling, past a bird lake and traditional-style Chinese garden, banyan court, lily pond, aviary, and—special this—sculpture walk, wherein you amble past works by ranking Hong Kong sculptors.

Tin Hau Temple (Temple Street) is one of a couple of dozen Hong Kong temples dedicated to Tin Hau, the goddess of sailors. The Temple Street temple is one of the oldest, and one of a quartet of neighboring places of worship in the Yau Ma Tei quarter. There are five principal altars, and as well—typically Hong Kong—the drum and bell that contributors sound when making gifts of money for the altars' lamp oil. You'll no doubt observe worshipers gently throwing wooden objects on the floor. Called *sing pui*, each has a flat and a rounded side. Landing on one side, it answers the worshiper's questions affirmatively; if the wood lands on its other side, the answer is a negative.

Wong Tai Sin Temple (a near-neighbor of the Kowloon Metro station taking its name, and but a couple of minutes distant) sees three million worshipers annually. It is at once modern (1973) and significant. No other temple makes so apparent its blend of the three major Hong Kong religions—Buddhism, Taoism, and Confucianism. And it's a looker, with the main building color-drenched in the traditional Chinese manner, with blue friezes and decorative elements in a variety of hues, the lot beneath a golden roof. Go inside to see the network of tables on which various offerings—joss sticks, fruit, various other foods—are left by worshipers who pray, the while making paper offerings, with fortune-tellers nearby.

THE NEW TERRITORIES

It is conceivable that the New Territories' title works against them—in the case of newcomers to Hong Kong. The name is, somehow, offputting with respect to tourism. And it is not all that accurate, since as long ago as the turn of the century—1898—China leased the area to Britain. The territories extend north from Kowloon to the Shum Chun River, which serves as the frontier with China, and they're more rural than urban.

For long sparsely populated, today much of the area has been developed—surprisingly lively small towns with high rises and teeming markets compete with rolling countryside, pretty beaches, traditional villages, and ranking temples. I recommend the Chinese University's Art Gallery on another page. But there's more to the New Territories, to wit:

Shatin —metropolis of the territories—typifies the substantial cities of the territories. Largely unknown abroad, with a population nearing three-quarters of a million, it is hardly without urban amenities, but there are other reasons for a visit, the range a popular racetrack, through *Ten Thousand Buddhas Monastery*, modern to be sure (it goes back less than half a century) and not easy of access (are you up to climbing close to five hundred steps?). If the answer is in the affirmative, your reward will be a vista not of ten thousand but actually of thirteen thousand Buddhas, the lot of them lining shelves within the monastery's main temple, with still another temple of the complex noted en route up the hill, and an additional quartet even higher up, beyond the principal building. *Po Fook Ancestral Hall* (adjacent to Ten Thousand Buddhas Monastery) opened in the early 1990s, and is a costly mix of mainly Tang but also Ming and Qing dynasty motifs, anchored on its Main Worship Hall and Pagoda, with a quartet of immense gold-leaf-surfaced Buddhas, carved-marble murals, and waterfalls in the garden.

Shatin's *Che Kung Temple*, away from the center in Tai Wai, goes back centuries, honoring a still revered general; note the bronze prayer wheel before the altar. *Shatin Racecourse* is state-of-the-art contemporary—justifiably the pride and joy of the Royal Hong Kong Jockey Club. Races take place weekend afternoons, September to June; if you're interested, ask at the Hong Kong Tourist Office how and where to buy tickets. Your passport is the only allowable identification. There's a tourist office tour, too. The Shatin management wisely takes advantage of the space ringed in by the track; it's the site of *Penfold Park*, a lovely bird sanctuary.

You'll do well to take in at least one fortified village typical of this area; *Tsang Tai Uk* is one such—fortified in the last century, with its symmetrical layout typical of area settlements—towers at each corner and parallel streets—in the center of which is an attractive courtyard.

Taipo —a good-sized city—has a pair of unusual temples. *Man Mo Temple* (Fu Shin Street) embraces a pair of structures, one on each side of its entrance. *Tin Hau Temple* (Ting Kok Road) honors a number of gods, each at a separate altar.

Bride's Pool Waterfalls (Bride's Pool Road) are romantically situated—in verdant forest—as well as being romantically named—after a legend in which a bride, en route to her wedding, fell from her sedan chair into the pool and drowned. (Bride's Pool Road is also the site of a visitor information center for the area.)

Tsuen Wan: Pay your respects at *Cheuk Lam Sin Yuen*, a relatively modern Buddhist monastery, with prime lures a trio of superb "Precious" Buddhas—the largest such in the territory. *Yuen Yuen* embraces a clutch of temples dedicated to Hong Kong's main religions—Buddhism, Confucianism, and Taoism, with the most architecturally superior of the temples based on a famed place of worship in the Chinese capital, Beijing.

Fanling is, at least with golfers, best known for the *Royal Hong Kong Golf Club*, a membership organization of course, but open weekdays to visitors, who must turn up in person to reserve times of play, and who will find clubs for rent; ask the Hong Kong Tourist Association for details. Fanling's *Luen Wo Market* is mornings-only (traditionally 10:30 to noon), with produce of course, but also local specialties, including the severe black hats local women wear.

San Tin: Man Clan Halls are onetime homes—locally designated as ancestral halls—of assorted families of the local Man Clan. Two stand out: *Man Shek Tong Hall* retains its eighteenth-century facade and interior, and *Man Lun-Fung Hall*—even older, with roots in the sixteenth century—is easily as visitable.

Kat Hing Wai is one of several walled villages that together constitute a larger area called Kam Tin. Kat Hing Wai is special, primarily because of the names of its inhabitants. It goes back to the seventeenth century, when its founders included a family called Tang; today there are literally hundreds of Tangs on scene. Note the eighteen-foot-high walls set off by a moat and punctuated by guardhouses; and hope that the village temple will be open so that you may inspect it.

Sai Kung is a New Territories town retaining enough of its centuries-old facade to attract visitors. Make a journey via sampan in the port. Take in *Tin Hau Temple*, rebuilt in 1878, but originally erected in the fourteenth century, with a noted inscribed rock to its rear.

Sheung Yiu is a onetime village—of considerable vintage—which, only a few decades back, lost the last of its residents (not that many remained) and became a museum, the exhibits embracing village houses chockablock with furnishings of the local Hakka people, and displays interpreting the Hakka life-style. Have a look.

Sheng Shui: Man Shek Tong is the name of what is called an ancestral hall—the elaborate ceremonial seat of a local clan, the Luis, that is eminently visitable. *Lok Ma Chau* (not infrequently shortened to "Look, Ma" by English-speaking visitors) is, to be sure, a lookout point—the view is of China—and worth knowing about for its rest rooms, if not

for the local women who want you to take their pictures—
and not for free. Go by car or taxi; public transport drops
you a half hour's walk away. *Tai Pu Tai* is a rich family's
house going back to the middle of the last century, whose
art is typical of the time and the place—dramatic murals
and statuary, behind a facade of brick and granite.

Clearwater Bay is the name of a scenic South China Sea
peninsula, with beaches its chief appeal. Nicest for swim-
mers and sunbathers is *Clearwater Bay Second Beach*. It has a
refreshment counter, changing facilities, even rowboats for
hire. This is a recommended spot for a break in the course
of area exploration.

Clearwater Bay Golf and Country Club (Saikung Peninsula) opens its doors—and its excellent facilities—to overseas visitors through the good offices of the Hong Kong
Tourist Association. There are eighteen holes of sporty
golf; tennis and badminton, squash and swimming, table
tennis and saunas—not to mention a clubhouse equipped
with both Chinese and Western restaurants and a cocktail
lounge. Golfers find clubs for rent at the club, as well as
rubber-soled shoes for tennis, squash, and badminton
courts. The appropriate phone numbers at Hong Kong
Tourist Association—to make arrangements for
Clearwater—are 801-7390 and 801-7292.

Joss House Bay: Tin Hau Temple is the successor to an originally eleventh-century structure, rebuilt a couple of centuries later, and the subject of a major restoration only a few
decades back. There's a pair of statues of the god of the title at the high altar, and the faithful make burnt offerings.
Hau Wong Temple and *Kwan Tai Temple* are nearby, both with
fine sculpture and ceramics mostly within, but on roofs
as well.

OFFSHORE ISLANDS

There are, as I have indicated on an earlier page, some 235 offshore islands. These include:

Lantau Island, twice the size of Hong Kong albeit with a population under twenty thousand in contrast to Hong Kong's million-plus, makes for a diverting excursion (although there's no doubt but that when Hong Kong's new international airport opens on Lantau, its laid-back charms can be expected to dissipate). Ferries leave frequently. (Hovercraft make the run in just over half an hour.) Lantau's peaks are largely responsible for its natural beauty. Traditional-style fishing villages are dotted about. There's good swimming at several south coast beaches, hearty hiking on well-marked paths, a perky principal town with a pair of names (*Silvermine Bay* or *Mui Wo*, take your pick), and unpretentious places to eat. The stilted town of *Tai O* (residents—mostly fishing families—live in elevated structures lining a stream that flows through it) is visitworthy, as are the *Tea Gardens,* the only plantations in the territory where tea is commercially cultivated (you may have a cup in the tearoom). Most fascinating for last: *Po Lin Monastery,* 2,500 feet skyward, in the mountains (there are buses from Silvermine Bay) and the principal Buddhist retreat in the territory, with three superb Buddha statues in its Main Pavilion, and what is said to be the world's largest outdoor representation of Buddha—completed as recently as 1990 and a hundred feet high.

Cheung Chau Island is good for exercise. By that I mean that cars are not allowed; you'll walk a lot, ideally devoting a full day to this island, cutting that time in half if you're pressed for time. Cheung Chau at its most splendid is *Pak Tai Temple,* dating back to the late eighteenth century, with treasures including statues of a pair of remarkable gen-

erals, each of whom was believed able to hear or see any-
thing regardless of distance. There's a sedan chair easily a
century old, used in ceremonial processions, a thousand-
year-old sword, and, biggest surprise: a clutch of smaller
statues of Pak Tai—the god of the north for whom the temple is named—each with a sculpted snake under one foot
and a sculpted turtle under the other.

Cheung Chau's public market—you want to go in the
morning—is among the more vibrant on the island, with
its range of wares dry goods and flowers to fruit and fish. If
you've always wanted to travel aboard a sampan, Cheung
Chay is the place. Proceed to the harbor, go aboard (boats
depart frequently), and select *Sai Wan*—site of Tin Hau
Temple—as your destination. Note, too, that this island's
beaches are good; that at *Tung Wan* is a leader, and with a
hotel, the Warwick, whose restaurant is an okay lunch
spot.

HONG KONG'S UNDERAPPRECIATED MUSEUMS

Museums in Hong Kong? On my early visits they were, as
far as I can recall, a virtually unknown quantity. Today,
with an invigorated—and invigorating—cultural life, its
museums have become a requisite feature of Hong Kong
exploration, with a special plus in their favor: none is
overly large. Here they are:

Art Gallery of the Institute of Chinese Studies (Chinese
University of Hong Kong, Shatin, New Territories) is a veritable gold mine of Chinese art and archeology, in clean-
lined contemporary quarters surrounding a reflecting pool
in a central courtyard, and with an annex for additional exhibits. There are beautiful things here—paintings and ink
drawings, hanging scrolls and illustrated leaves for al-
bums, rubbings from temple inscriptions, deftly decorated
tiles from before the Christian era, mirrors of bronze dat-

ing back two thousand years, venerable pottery, and exquisitely carved jade. If you've time for but one museum, this
should be it. And not only the museum is handsome, so is
the entire university campus.

Fung Ping Shan Museum (University of Hong Kong, 94
Bonham Road, Hong Kong): My Fung Ping Shan notes
brim with exclamation points. This is a striking circular repository for beautiful Chinese artisanship that in less than
four decades has grown to a collection of some seven hundred pieces—a bronze brooch from the fourteenth century,
a Ming celadon trio of vases from the sixteenth century,
porcelain plates a century younger, eighteenth-century lacquer fashioned into boxes and saucers and pillows and
bowls, seventeenth-century Tang horses, thirteenth-
century Buddha heads, and, as well, mirrors of bronze as
old as the third century. Take your time here, and stroll
around the campus; it's handsome.

Flagstaff House Museum of Tea Ware (Cotton Tree Drive,
Central, Hong Kong): If the Art Gallery (above) is the most
requisite of museums, the Flagstaff is surely the most
charming. Start with its setting: an 1844 house that's the
oldest Western-style structure in Hong Kong. When you
visit, you get an idea of what domestic architecture was
like at that period, and simultaneously—and effortlessly—
you gain a bit of background on the history of tea and tea
ware from behind the facade of colonnaded mansion. The
practice of tea-drinking from the third century onward is
what this museum is all about: the great Ming era of teapot
manufacture, later Qing pieces, beyond into this century,
the range simplicity to elegance.

Hong Kong Museum of Art (Hong Kong Cultural Centre,
Kowloon) runs a wide gamut—Chinese paintings and calligraphy, ceramics (including extraordinary Qing Dynasty

painted porcelains) and jade, bronzes and lacquer, exquisitely carved bamboo and ivory, furniture extending over a period of many centuries. The range is from, say, a brown-pottery teapot dating to the sixteenth century with lines so severe it could be of contemporary manufacture, through to say, polychrome wooden figures from the thirteenth century, and contemporary scrolls as well.

Hong Kong Museum of History (Haiphong Road, Kowloon) is a repository of old objects, venerable documents, archaeological treasures, and graphic photos, the better to give us an idea of what Hong Kong was like before our time. This important museum operates several satellites (below).

Hong Kong Railway Museum (Taipo Market Railway Station) is visitable for its lovingly preserved original waiting room, ticket offices, and signal cabin. There are antique coaches, too, and a gallery of railway exhibits. Lots of fun for buffs.

Hong Kong Science Museum (2 Science Museum Road, Kowloon): The territory's newest museum occupies the four levels of an extraordinary building that opened in 1991. Most amusing section is the Kid Zone, admired by visitors considerably older than the 3-to-7 group for whom it is intended. The transportation area's prime exhibit is Cathay Pacific Airways' original plane, a 1942 DC-3 suspended in midair as if in flight. The energy machine, in the museum's 60-foot-high atrium, is the center of the action, with a computer lab, a fascinating exhibit based on types of transportation, and still another exhibit on home appliances among highlights.

Hong Kong Space Museum (10 Salisbury Road, Kowloon): A space museum in Hong Kong? Why not? Its Planetarium is one of the world's largest. It blends museum-type exhibits, including a display of what Mars might be like two centuries hence, with a series of shows, each with its own performance times and admission fees.

Law Uk Folk Museum (14 Kut Shing Street, Hong Kong)—a unit of the Hong Kong Museum of History (above) is an eighteenth-century house—the only such structure remaining in its neighborhood, with the pluses of a well-documented history and ownership by generations of a single family. To observe are the entrance hall, sitting rooms, and kitchen of the main floor, the lot furnished in the style of the early twentieth century.

Lei Tung Uk Museum (a branch of the Hong Kong Museum of History, above, located at 41 Tonkin Street, Kowloon) is an ancient tomb, which preserves within its brick walls a series of four chambers laid out in the form of a cross; three are barrel-vaulted, with the fourth—the first as you enter—dome-topped. To be seen are three score funerary objects—pottery vessels, bronzes, even models of barns and houses, the lot presumed to be from the period of the first through third centuries A.D. And note: Lei Tung Uk was discovered as recently as 1955.

Lei Cheng Uk Museum (Kowloon Park) is chockablock with rubbings from a tomb illustrating daily life during the long-ago Han era, not to mention bits and pieces from the tomb. You want to make a visit if only to give yourself an idea of how very, very old Hong Kong and its surroundings are. A worthy division of the Hong Kong Museum of History.

Police Museum (near Park Road bus station, Hong Kong) occupies a onetime police station and police buffs miss it at their peril. It tells the story of the Royal Hong Kong Police

Force from 1844 onward, and sets forth an introductory history of Hong Kong. There's a gallery for short-term exhibits. Lots of fun.

Sam Tung Uk Museum (Kwu Uk Lane, Tsuen Wan, New Territories) goes back a couple of centuries—to the time when it was a walled village. When villagers were relocated in modern quarters some years back, the old village was restored and opened as a museum in 1987. This was the seat of a wealthy family, which is apparent by the elaborate detail of its houses and their interiors—fine lanterns, an ancestral altar, furniture, and fittings.

Tai Fu Tai House Museum (Yuen Long, New Territories) is a mansion turned museum, constructed more than a century back by a local fat cat. The title translates as Important Person's House. Take in the entrance hall, sittings rooms, and the big main hall.

3

Hong Kong to Stay

THE HOTEL SCENE

Hong Kong has a number of natural attributes: the accident of geography that placed it at the southern tip of China; the waters of the South China Sea that lap at its coast, delineating Hong Kong Island; a generally equable climate; and—hardly insignificant—proximity to continental Asia and the South Pacific.

But it's as a crossroads that Hong Kong achieved status. Its visitors are en route to or from China, off to or arriving from Japan, Thailand, the Philippines, Australia, Europe, or the Americas. My point is that sheltering travelers has for long been a Hong Kong industry. The makers and shakers know that their most important asset—after location—is hotels.

No other geographical space as compact as this one—anywhere—does better by hotels. Their design, construction, decoration, maintenance, staffing, and management are, as a group, unsurpassed planet-wide. Of course there are exceptions; I don't warrant that you'll not have a problem or a less than lovely room or faulty service upon occasion. Generally, though, the standard is extraordinary, with many of the international hotel chains on scene, and some stellar independents, as well.

Bear in mind that hotels are located in quantity—both on Hong Kong Island (whose chief urban area is officially termed Victoria, but is mostly called Hong Kong, with its downtown dubbed "Central") and, with equally strong representation in the mainland area of Kowloon, a ferry ride or underground motor-tunnel trek across the harbor. You're conveniently situated on either side, both of which are popular with visitors. What follows alphabetically is a selection of hotels in each of these two principal areas, categorized, as is the case in all the books of my series as *Luxury, First Class,* or *Moderate.* And note: Hong Kong is invariably busy and visitor-filled; reserve your hotel in advance.

HONG KONG ISLAND

Asia Hotel (1 Wang Tak Street, in the Happy Valley area of Hong Kong; phone 574-9922), though away from the action, is worth knowing about if what you seek is an agreeable, relatively small house. There are 111 doubles and a few suites, as well as a Chinese restaurant and bar. *Moderate.*

Cheung Chau Warwick Hotel (East Bay, Cheung Chau Island) is popular with Hong Kongers who want to get away from the city's bustle for a spell, on one of the offshore islands. Location is beachfront. Both Western and Chinese cuisine; bar-lounge, and—nice touch, this—balconies attached to all 67 rooms. *First Class.*

China Merchants Hotel (160 Connaught Road West, Hong Kong, phone 559-6886) is, to be sure, popular with Chinese business travelers, but the rest of us are welcome too. Both Western and Chinese restaurants, bar-lounge. *Moderate.*

Conrad Hotel (Pacific Place, 88 Queensway, Hong Kong; phone 521-3838). If you haven't been following Hilton Hotels' nomenclature changes, it is perhaps worth noting that the original Hilton Hotels USA are all situated within the U.S., that Hilton International Hotels are, by and large, outside the U.S. (except for a subcategory dubbed Vista, in certain American cities), and that Hilton Hotels USA in recent seasons has also gone abroad, *but* under the guise of the Conrad chain, named, of course, for the founding father, the late Conrad Hilton. So much for terminology. Hong Kong's Conrad is a 61-story tower that's part of a complex known as Pacific Place in the Central business district. Public spaces—beige-toned, picture-window lobby, comfortable cocktail lounges where you sink into club chairs—are welcoming. There's a quartet of top-of-the-line restaurants (range is Italian through Cantonese), and they're detailed on later pages. When you consider that this is a modern house (new hotels too often tend to create capacious public spaces but small bedrooms), those of the 513 contemporarily styled guest rooms I have inspected or inhabited are surprisingly capacious, with utterly fabulous views from higher up. And service, again in my experience, is super. *Luxury.*

Evergreen International Hotel (33 Hennessy Road in Wanchau; phone 866-9111) is a branch of a Taiwan-based chain, whose emphasis is good value. There's a trio of restaurants (Chinese, Japanese, Western) and of bars, swimming pool, health club, and a business center. Those of the 357 rooms I've inspected are small but attractive; there are phones in all the baths, and the 35 junior suites—bigger than the standard rooms—are good buys. A gratis hotel-operated shuttle bus links the Evergreen to Central. *Moderate.*

Excelsior Hotel (Causeway Bay, Hong Kong; phone 894-8888) is adjacent to the World Trade Center and convenient to department stores and other shops, not to mention an adjacent station of Hong Kong's MTR, or subway. Ask for an elevated room (there are more than 900 all told) for a smashing harbor view. Furnishings are attractive, a modern-traditional mix that works well. The Excelsior has seven restaurants, all of them Western, none Chinese, with a spectacularly situated Penthouse Lounge. A link of the Mandarin Oriental chain that's a member of Leading Hotels of the World. Very nice. *Luxury.*

Furama Kempinski Hotel (1 Connaught Road, Hong Kong; phone 525-5111): I first became acquainted with the Kempinski chain in the course of researching *Germany at Its Best*; this is a group affiliated with Lufthansa German Airlines, and in my experience it's top rank. The conveniently situated Hong Kong outpost is core of the business district with 523 attractive, thoughtfully equipped rooms (ask for either a Peak-view or slightly pricier harbor-view room, as high as you can get). There are spiffy suites, too. And no less than seven restaurants, the range Chinese through French. *Luxury.*

Garden View International House (1 Macdonnell Road, Hong Kong; phone 877-3737) occupies a white circular tower, is affiliated with the YWCA but unisex, and has among its accommodations 130 rooms (minimums are small but okay) and a couple of dozen good-sized suites on upper floors, from which there's a nice view of the white mansion that's Government House, the governor's official residence. There's a coffee shop and guests may use the

Y's gym and pool. The zoo and botanical garden are easy strolls away. A good deal. *Moderate.*

Grand Hyatt Hotel (1 Harbour Road, Hong Kong; phone 861-1234) is one of two Hyatts in Hong Kong, and not to be confused with the *Hyatt Regency Hong Kong,* on Nathan Road in Kowloon. The Grand is polished marble and silvered glass without, Art Deco 1930s style in its interior spaces. A whopping 70 percent of the 573 handsome rooms and suites are harbor-view. The swimming pool is the largest free-form pool in Hong Kong and there are rooftop tennis courts. The premium-tabbed, extra-amenity Regency Club occupies seven floors, with its own pool. Grissini (which I review in the succeeding chapter) is the Italian restaurant. One Harbour Road is split-level Cantonese, and you want to have afternoon tea—if not a drink—at the Tiffin Lounge during your stay. Special. *Luxury.*

Grand Plaza Hotel (2 Kornhill Road, Quarry Bay, Hong Kong; phone 886-0011) is nothing if not interestingly located. It straddles the top of the Tai Koo station of the Mass Transit Railway, from which it's relatively easy to gain the center of Hong Kong Island, some distance away. This is a relatively recent house, with close to 350 rooms and suites, each as modern as can be, with the top four floors—18th through 22nd—devoted to suites and served by special elevators. There are two restaurants (including a coffee shop), several drinking parlors, a fitness center, indoor badminton courts, and an indoor pool with an adjacent deck for stretching out in the sun. And, bless the Grand Plaza: it has emulated U.S. hotels, with ice-cube machines on every floor. Another plus: immense Kornhill Plaza shopping mall is adjacent. *First Class.*

Harbour Hotel (116 Gloucester Road in the Wanchai district; phone 574-8211) is a budget-stretcher, with 200 okay rooms, Chinese restaurant and bar. *Moderate.*

Hong Kong Hilton Hotel (2 Queen's Road, Central, Hong Kong; phone 523-3111): Three Hong Kong hotels hold special memories for me: the Peninsula (below), because it was the hotel of my very first trip many years back (and is to this day world-class); the Regent, whose utter luxury, style, and elegance were in such stark contrast to a succession of hotels in China—a decade back—from which I had just arrived; and the Hong Kong Hilton, where I first stayed some years ago en route home with colleagues covering the official opening of the then Manila Hilton—a group, as I look back, that included Lis Brewer, then Hilton International's New York-based whiz of a public relations director; Ila Stanger, then with *Harper's Bazaar* and now head honcho at *Travel & Leisure*; TV *Kaleidoscope's* still fast-traveling Dale Remington; Kermit Holt, then travel editor of the *Chicago Tribune*; and a trio of much-missed friends— the late Marion Gough of *House Beautiful*; the late John McLeod of the now defunct *Washington Star*; and the late Leavitt Morris of the *Christian Science Monitor*. Well, enough nostalgia! The point about the Hilton is that, along with the Mandarin Oriental (below) it predated the brilliant clutch of skyscrapers that now constitute one of the planet's most distinguished skylines. The Hilton must remain grateful to its architects, Palmer and Turner, for designing a building that remains a stunner. Its 26 stories embrace 760 guest rooms and suites and no less than nine restaurants and bars, some of which I evaluate in a later chapter. The original cost—U.S. $14 million—a lot at the time. But the late 1980s saw an additional U.S. $20 million expended on a stem-to-stern refurbishing, including all guest rooms, restaurants, and public areas, and the addition of a trio of tennis courts to complement the fitness center and swimming pool. The half dozen highest-up stories are Executive Floors with separate check-in and a range of special facilities, including complimentary breakfast, afternoon tea, and cocktails, not to mention loans of portable phones—today's ultimate status symbol. And there's a Hilton bonus: the hotel has its own yacht, *Wan Fu*, with a range of daytime, cocktail, and dinner cruises. *Luxury.*

Island Shangri-La Hongkong Hotel (Pacific Place, 88 Queensway, Central, Hong Kong, phone 877-3838): Pull up to this newer of Hong Kong's Shangri-La hotels from the proper perspective and you utter but one expletive upon seeing its tall, lipstick-shaped exterior: Wow! The Shangri-La's tower contains 566 rooms (including precisely three dozen suites) all with electrical outlets for personal computers and fax machines, traditional decor in tones of gold and beige, with plenty of work surface on writing tables. There are five restaurants; take your choice of three Western-style (including a coffee shop), Chinese, and Japanese; and a trio of bars, one edging the swimming pool. *Luxury.*

J. W. Marriott Hotel (Pacific Place, 88 Queensway, Central, Hong Kong, phone 810-8366) makes its home in a stunner of a 41-story tower, with its 605 rooms and suites occupying the 27 upper floors of the building, its lobby—three stories in height—dominated by cascading waterfalls framed by marble and glass. Guest rooms I've inspected stand out for size (they tend to be big) with computerized bedside controls for curtains, lights, and the like, and stunning black marble baths, each with its own stall shower to complement the tub, and all with terrycloth robes for guests' use. There are three Executive Floors, premium-tabbed, with breakfast and cocktails served in their lounges; an up-to-the-minute business center, half a dozen restaurants (both Chinese and Western) and lounges, a honey of an outdoor pool along with steam rooms, sauna, massage rooms, and a health center. Service, in my experience, is smiling and skilled. *Luxury.*

Luk Kwok Hotel (72 Gloucester Road in the Wanchai section of Hong Kong; phone 866-2166): You are tempted, if you're an English-speaker, to dub the Luk Kwok the Look Quick. It's gracefully clean-lined, with 200 rooms occupying the 19th through 29th floors of a central high rise. Standard rooms can be small; those in the deluxe category are bigger. But all rooms have three phones and are done in soft pastels. There are both Cantonese and Western restaurants, and a business center. *First Class.*

Mandarin Oriental Hotel (5 Connaught Road, Central, Hong Kong; phone 522-0111): Two points worth pondering about the Mandarin Oriental: First is that General Manager G. C. Balneari's staff numbers 1,100—virtually double the number of rooms. (The premium-category, extra-amenity Mandarin Floors are special.) Second is that two sides of the hotel afford vistas of the Hong Kong harbor. One of the pioneer luxury hostelries, the Mandarin's rooms tend to be big, and most have balconies. All are with recently renovated marble baths. Suites—big Presidential but others, too, are sumptuous. You like the look of the place from the moment you step into the black marble lobby, with its gold temple carvings. There are French, Cantonese, and Western restaurants (evaluated on succeeding pages) as well as a coffee shop and a quartet of bar-lounges, with additional facilities ranging from barbershop/beauty salon through health and business centers, swimming pool, and solarium. Member, Leading Hotels of the World. *Luxury.*

New Harbour Hotel (41 Hennessy Road, in the Wanchai section of Hong Kong; phone 861-1166, and not to be confused with the New World Harbour View, below) is relatively small by Hong Kong standards, with just 173 rooms, mostly twins or doubles; 15 are suites. There are both Chinese and Western restaurants, and a bar. *Moderate.*

New World Harbour View Hotel (1 Harbour Road in the Wanchai section of Hong Kong; phone 866-2288)—just opposite the Grand Hyatt, (above) is a formidable high rise, essentially contemporary albeit with traditional touches—like Regency- and Louis XVI-style furnishings in some of the public spaces. The higher up of the 862 rooms (corner suites especially) afford picture-book views, and baths are an elegant mix of teak and marble, but with tiny cakes of soap, more's the pity. Four upper floors constitute the Dynasty Club, with premium tabs and extra amenities. There's a trio of eateries, as many bar-lounges, business center, and a swimming pool that is shared with the neighboring Hyatt. One could wish for a warmer ambience at the New World Harbour View. But there's no denying that it's full-facility. *Luxury.*

Park Lane Hotel (310 Gloucester Road in the Causeway Bay section of Hong Kong; phone 890-3355) is modern and much-marbled in its public spaces, with 850 well-equipped rooms (aim to be high up in one of the suites, if your budget will allow it); it has a pair of Western restaurants and cocktail lounge among its many facilities. *Luxury.*

Ramada Inn Hong Kong (61 Lockhart Road in the Wanchai section of Hong Kong; phone 861-1000), not to be confused with Ramada Inn Kowloon across the harbor (below), is reasonably central and near a subway station. There are

335 well-equipped rooms and suites, coffee shop and bar. *First Class.*

Ritz Carlton Hotel (89 Queensway, Hong Kong; phone 526-5031), though recent (it opened in 1991) happily re- tains all of the typical Ritz features—and adds some. Loca- tion is heart of Central, extending over an entire city block edging the snazzy Hong Kong Club, with views, depend- ing on the side of the building and the height of your room—of Victoria Peak, the harbor, or Kowloon. This is not an overlarge house. There are just 216 rooms, including a pair of presidential suites and 27 smaller suites, with a premium-tab club floor offering continental breakfast, afternoon tea, and hors d'oeuvres with cocktails served on the house in the evening. Rooms feature marble baths- cum-phone and terry robes. There's a fitness center with an outdoor pool, French fare in the smart Dining Room, the bigger Ritz Restaurant overlooking the harbor, both Chinese and Japanese eateries as well, and a pair of bars. *Luxury.*

Victoria Hotel (Shun Tak Centre, 200 Connaught Road, Central, Hong Kong; phone 540-7228): You're conveniently located here in an ever-so-contemporary complex, with scarlet-accented exteriors. There are 534 full-facility rooms, a half dozen suites, and a quartet of restaurants: Ameri- can, Cantonese, continental, and grill room. Plus both swimming pool and health center. *Luxury.*

KOWLOON

Ambassador Hotel (26 Nathan Road, Kowloon; phone 366- 6321) is an agreeable 313-room house whose rooms and suites (those I've inspected are really capacious) were treated to relatively recent renovations, both tasteful and thorough, with white marble counters a feature of the baths. The Ambassador Club occupies three floors, with premium tabs inclusive of breakfast, cocktails, and after-dinner wine and cheese. Nice. *Luxury.*

Eaton Hotel (380 Nathan Road, Kowloon; phone 782-1818) is a modern-as-can-be house that opened in 1990, with just under 400 nicely planned rooms, both Chinese and Western restaurants, and a cocktail lounge. Pleasant. *First Class.*

Fortuna Hotel (355 Nathan Road, Kowloon; phone 385-1011) has 187 warm-look rooms, many good-sized, a reliable Chinese restaurant, and a bar. *Moderate.*

Grand Hotel (14 Carnarvon Road, Kowloon; phone 366-9331) is contemporarily styled in pastel tones, with nearly 200 rooms including a quartet of suites, and a restaurant whose kicker is an international buffet. *Moderate.*

Grand Tower Hotel (627 Nathan Road, Kowloon; phone 789-0011) is a perfectly nice-looking hotel—and fairly big, too, with 545 rooms. The superior-category accommodations are decent size, but standard rooms—at least those I have inspected—are small, although all baths have Jacuzzi tubs. Withal, a hotel built as recently as 1987 should have facilities to prevent garlicky kitchen odors in the lobby and corridors (there are several restaurants). Because of smelly public spaces in the course of my inspection, I can't recommend this one. *First Class.*

Holiday Inn Golden Mile (46 Nathan Road, Kowloon; phone 369-3111) is one of a pair of this chain in Kowloon. Both are about the same size: just under 600 rooms, both with pools and gyms. The Golden Mile has Chinese and German restaurants and a tempting deli as well as a bar, and is somewhat less expensive than the Harbour View (below). *First Class.*

Holiday Inn Harbour View (70 Mody Road, Kowloon; phone 721-5161) offers to feed hungry guests (and hungry transients as well), in a network of restaurants serving American, Chinese, French, Italian, and Japanese cuisine. There are just under 600 pleasant rooms. *First Class.*

Imperial Hotel (3 Nathan Road, Kowloon; phone 366-2201) is well situated, with 219 okay rooms, most of them doubles, and an international restaurant. *Moderate.*

Kimberley Hotel (Kimberley Road, Kowloon; phone 723-3888) is a pleasant, relatively new hotel, close to Nathan Road shops, with nearly 500 well-equipped rooms, of which 76 are kitchen-equipped suites in the Kimberley Tower. Restaurants, bar. *First Class.*

Kowloon Hotel (19 Nathan Road, Kowloon; phone 369-8698) stands out first because of its striking glass facade, and as well for inviting interior spaces, the range a big marble-accented lobby through to the guest rooms and suites, 737 all told. I must caution you, though, that standard rooms and their baths are small; superior category accommodations are more spacious. Still, 60 rooms (all harbor-view) are computer-equipped. There's a business center, ice-cube machines in each floor's corridor, terry robes and slippers for all guests, as well as super amenity-packed guest toilet kits in bathrooms. Meal choices? There's a coffee shop, Chinese and Italian restaurants. But I save the Kowloon's unique-in-Hong Kong feature for last. Ask at the desk, upon departing for a taxi ride to a destination with which you're not familiar, for a slip that will indicate where you're going in both Chinese and English, along with instructions in Chinese for the cabbie. The Kowloon is operated by the same company that runs the Peninsula (below). *First Class.*

Kowloon Shangri-La Hotel (64 Mody Road, Kowloon; phone 721-2111) is, I must point out, at the eastern end of Kowloon, a good ten-minute walk to Nathan Road. Withal, it's a full-facility, 719-room house, and those of its doubles and suites I have inspected are smart and generously proportioned. The premium-category, extra-tab Club 21 includes airport pickup, breakfast, and cocktails. And there are five restaurants; I evaluate Chinese-cuisine Shang Palace in the succeeding chapter, but there are, as well, Margaux (Western), Nadaman (Japanese), Steak Place, and a coffee shop, as well as several bar-lounges, one on the roof. *Luxury.*

New Astor Hotel (11 Carnarvon Road, Kowloon; phone 366-7261) is well placed—just off Nathan Road—with 150 okay rooms, and a Chinese-Western restaurant. Good value. *Moderate.*

New World Hotel (22 Salisbury Road, Kowloon; phone 369-4111) is attached to the fabulous 400-shop-apartment-office tower complex whose name it takes. A recent and major refurbishing reduced the number of rooms from 729 to 550 (each room is now a third larger), with new baths, plus the premium-tab Dynasty Club occupying several floors. There are three restaurants and as many bars, and an outdoor pool. Withal, the ambience lacks warmth and charm. *Luxury.*

Nikko Hong Kong Hotel (72 Mody Road; phone 739-1111) is the local link of a Japan-based chain. There are 461 pleasant rooms, and restaurants featuring not only Japanese cuisine, but Chinese and Western food, too. Health center and swimming pool. *First Class.*

Omni Hong Kong Hotel (Harbour City, Kowloon; phone 736-0088) is one of several Hong Kong hostelries bearing the Omni name. It's distinguished for handsome interiors—decor is essentially traditional—with especially smart suites (see—or, better yet, book—the Presidential, if you're able)—and a pair of floors—Continental by name—with complimentary breakfasts and cocktails. But standard accommodations in this 720-room house are pleasant, too, at least those I've inspected. This hotel boasts a veritable Restaurant Row—with eateries devoted to Western cuisine, Cantonese specialties, Japanese fare, and a coffee shop where buffets, breakfast through dinner, are notable. The business center is well equipped, and guests may hold meetings without charge in the board room. *Luxury.*

Omni Marco Polo Hotel (Harbour City, Kowloon; phone 736-0888) is considerably smaller and somewhat less expensive than the Omni Hong Kong, above (the Marco Polo has 400 rooms and suites) and has Western but no Oriental restaurants. Cocktail lounge. *First Class.*

Omni Prince Hotel (Harbour City, Canton Road, Kowloon; phone 736-1888)—smallest in room count (401) of the Omni trio—is also the least expensive, although not by all that much. Half a hundred of the rooms are suites. The Rib Room specializes in steaks and roast beef; there's a coffee shop, as well, and a pair of bar-lounges. Pleasant. *First Class.*

Park Hotel (61 Chatham Road South, Kowloon; phone 366-1371) is good-sized (there are just over 400 rooms, of which close to 40 are suites), with both Western and Cantonese cuisine in its restaurant, and a bar. *Moderate.*

Peninsula Hotel (Salisbury Road, Kowloon; phone 366-6251): The Peninsula is synonymous with Hong Kong. It was what lured me to Hong Kong on my first visit a quarter century back. And it's been a Hong Kong headquarters on each succeeding visit. Opened in 1928 (with its next-door neighbor at the time a long-since-razed YMCA) it has mellowed beautifully, improving with age, thanks to a razor-sharp maintenance program and its management's conviction that it has a global reputation to maintain. I suspect a principal secret of its success—along with the skills of Swiss General Manager Felix Bieger and a crackerjack management team at the helm—is that it has remained small. The 158 rooms and suites of the original, still very-much-in-use building were supplemented only in the early 1990s with an addition that brings the room count to 300—still a modest total for one of the world's great hotels. It goes without saying that you want to reserve as far in advance as possible. No matter your room, count on a fabulous marble bath, fax machine, and video-laser disc players, even special connections for personal computers, with messages for you delivered via TV (with a copy of each message at Reception). Staff is pegged at three employees per room. The facade of the Peninsula—it could be a great British mansion—has remained essentially unchanged over the years. The lobby, which extends the length of the main floor, doubles as Hong Kong's No. 1 congregating spot for tea or coffee or a drink, with breakfast service and good things to eat the day and evening long. No two rooms or suites are quite alike, although you want to be as high up as possible, facing Salisbury Road and the harbor. With its heart-of-Kowloon situation, the Peninsula's restaurants keep busy. I evaluate them—Gaddi's, the most celebrated; Chesa, in my experience one of the best Swiss restaurants outside of Switzerland (see *Switzerland at Its Best*); Spring Moon (Chinese) and Lobby—in the chapter following. There are other Peninsula pluses: eight chauffeur-driven Rolls-Royces for lease by the hour or the day (as well as, of course, self-drive cars), boats for harbor tours and parties, even a helicopter service. And let me conclude with another Peninsula plus.

So far as I can tell, this was the first Hong Kong hotel positioning an attendant on each floor, at your beck and call, at a desk near the elevators to greet you upon each arrival and smile good-bye whenever you depart. A Peninsula Group hotel that's a member of Leading Hotels of the World. *Luxury.*

Ramada Inn Kowloon (73 Chatham Road South, Kowloon; phone 311-1100—and to be confused with neither the Ramada Renaissance, below, nor the Ramada Inn Hong Kong, above) is situated a hop and a skip from shops of Nathan Road and Star Ferry Terminal, for the crossing to Hong Kong Island. This is a nice-looking house, with 205 amenity-filled rooms; a restaurant, Café Society, that's good-looking and with good things to eat; and a bar-lounge. *First Class.*

Ramada Renaissance Hotel (8 Peking Road, Kowloon; phone 311-3311) is one of the most attractive of the upscale division of the Ramada group that I've come across. You're impressed with the quiet good looks of the arched-ceiling lobby and its cocktail lounge. There are four restaurants— Capriccio (among the city's better Italian eateries), Tang Court (Cantonese), Bostonian (seafood), and Sun's Café. The business center is well equipped and the Renaissance Club is the premium-tab area, with fax in each room, and breakfast and afternoon tea on the house. *Luxury.*

Regal Airport Hotel (Sa Po Road, adjacent to Hong Kong International Airport, with which it is connected by an elevated over-the-highway walkway; phone 718-0333) is worth knowing about if you arrive in Hong Kong late in the day and must depart—more's the pity—early the next morning. There are 400 soundproof rooms, with those in the superior category very nice indeed. Airport arrivals and departures are indicated on the screen of each room's

TV. There are good dining options: snazzy Five Continents seafood house, and coffee shop, with a trio of bar-lounges. *First Class.*

Regal Meridien Hotel (71 Mody Road, Kowloon; phone 722-1818): I initially encountered the Regal Meridien in the course of a dinner in its Restaurant de France (below), which was so good that I returned to inspect the rest of the hotel. Those of the 600 rooms (including 33 suites) that I looked over are indeed pleasant, with big baths a highlight. The Rendezvous cocktail lounge is kicky, and La Brasserie, the second restaurant, is Gallic-influenced. *First Class.*

Regent Hotel (Salisbury Road, Kowloon; phone 721-1211): If you exited China a decade back as I did—before it was chockablock with comfortable hotels as it is today—and you headed for the luxury of the Regent, you never stop being grateful for the happy contrast. When Regent International planned this Hong Kong flagship, they wisely hired the noted American architectural firm of Skidmore, Owings and Merrill (in collaboration with Joseph Chan and interior designer Don Siembieda) to create what is one of Asia's handsomest hostelries. With appropriately astute service to match. Although he was still at the famed Brenner's Park Hotel in Germany's Baden-Baden when I first met him, Thomas Axmacher is now general manager of the Regent—and operates it with style and charm. You're heart of Kowloon here; ideally you want a high-floor room (there are 602, seven of them stunning suites) for a vista of the harbor. Surfaced in red granite, with considerable space given to picture windows, the Regent takes full advantage of its situation. Accommodations—those I've inhabited and inspected—are generous-sized and with exceptional baths—Italian marble with sunken tubs and glass-enclosed shower stalls, as well as sunken Jacuzzi tubs and steam showers in baths of the suites, on the terraces of some of which—talk about opulence—there are Jacuzzi pools with harbor views. The hotel's swimming pool is framed by a landscaped terrace. The Lobby Lounge—several stories high and with glass walls on the harbor side—is a principal Hong Kong congregating spot, while its mezzanine counterpart is kicky in the evening, with live entertainment and dancing. There's a health spa. And the quartet of restaurants is exceptional; I evaluate the top three—Plume (Western), Lai Ching Heen (Cantonese), and the Steak House on later pages. The fourth, big and bustling Harbourside, takes honors with me, certainly, as the town's top hotel coffee shop. Member, Leading Hotels of the World. *Luxury.*

Royal Garden Hotel (69 Mody Road, Kowloon; phone 721-5215): You don't forget the Royal Garden. Not, at least, after you've had a look at its spectacular 100-foot-high landscaped atrium-lobby, accented with waterfalls and ponds, tall trees and verdant ferns, with a cocktail lounge (there's piano music in the evening) center stage. Those of the nearly 400 rooms I've inspected are by no means anticlimactic. Forty of these (some duplex with winding staircases) are especially handsome, but standard rooms are attractive, too, with baths tiptop. I'm partial to the Falcon Pub-Disco for a roast beef lunch or dinner. But formal Lalique is tastily French, and buffets are copious in the Greenery. Member, Leading Hotels of the World. *Luxury.*

Royal Pacific Hotel (33 Canton Road, atop the China Hong Kong City shopping mall; phone 736-1188) is at once central, contemporary, and a footbridge away from the ferry for Hong Kong. This is a modern, 632-room-and-suite house, whose designers have made good use of color and pattern in the interiors. Switzerland's fondue is a specialty of the Chalet Restaurant, and there are a coffee shop and bar, as well as a fitness center. *First Class.*

Sheraton Hong Kong Hotel (20 Nathan Road; phone 369-1111) is a long-on-scene but modernized house with just under a thousand rooms, business center, health club/pool, several restaurants (one specializes in U.S. steaks) and bars. Groups are a specialty. *Luxury.*

4

Hong Kong to Eat and Drink

"C" IS FOR COSMOPOLITAN

My verdict on Hong Kong's hotels (Chapter 3) is as enthusiastic as on hostelries of other great destinations—London, Paris, Rome, New York, Hawaii, and Switzerland to name some—but I am no less enthusiastic in evaluating Hong Kong's restaurants.

What is so extraordinary about what looks like no more than a dot on the map is that it has developed into one of the planet's most cosmopolitan—and at the same time, delicious—concentrations of restaurants. They total in the thousands and those that are Chinese are infinitely more common than, say, the ubiquitous coffee shops of New York.

But Hong Kong does not rest on the laurels of Chinese food despite the fact that—along with those of France and Italy—it is one of the three great world cuisines. The restaurant scene is as much a mixed bag as the population—predominantly Chinese to be sure, but with exceptional representation of French and Italian restaurants, American and Japanese as well, along with Indian, Austrian and German, steak and rib, Swiss and Indonesian, Thai and Korean, Mexican and English.

And I should make clear—and will elaborate in this chapter on restaurants, that all of the principal cuisines of China are represented in Hong Kong. Cantonese, of course, because Hong Kong is in the neighborhood of Guangdong, the Chinese province whose chief city is Guangzhou—formerly Canton. Withal, Hong Kong is a place to become acquainted with such specialties as Chiu Chow, Hangzhou, Hunan, Beijing (still frequently referred to, culinarily, as Peking), Shanghai, Szechuan (which in Hong Kong is spelled Sichuan), and Taiwanese. A nice way to gain acquaintance with the Chinese cuisines is to lunch daily in a Chinese restaurant and dine in a Western restaurant (or vice versa). Caveat: Be sure to reserve (I indicate phone numbers for all restaurants in this chapter), especially for the midday meal in Chinese restaurants—the big meal of the day for Chinese businesspeople. Still another caveat: Do *not* eschew hotel restaurants. Do remember that hotel eateries are patronized by the community at large—by no means only by hotel guests; I cannot be too emphatic about this point. By and large, it's the successful hotel restaurants—integral operations in leading hotels, many of them links of top-rank international chains, that can afford to import A-1 foreign chefs for their non-Chinese restaurants and employ especially skilled Chinese chefs, too, as well as experienced maîtres d'hôtel, captains, and waiters, not to mention talented interior designers for their restaurants, Chinese as well as foreign. I don't want to imply that there are no good independent restaurants outside of hotels; of course there are—lots of them, with a number evaluated on these pages. It's only that Hong Kong's hotel dining rooms are special and I don't want you to miss out on at least a representative sampling of them.

What follows is a selected group of restaurants separated by category, in the same three price ranges I use in all my *World at Its Best* guides: *Luxury, First Class,* and *Moderate.*

AFTERNOON TEA

You are, of course, on British soil, so that the British custom of afternoon tea is widespread—and can be quite as delightful as on home turf. A few suggestions:

Greenery (Royal Garden Hotel, Mody Road, Kowloon; phone 721-5215) is a veritable tropical garden adjoining the hotel's stunner of an atrium. The good news about its tea is that it's buffet style; you can be quite as greedy as you like, helping yourself to scones and sandwiches, pastry and waffles, crêpes and pies. Friendly. *First Class.*

Lobby (Peninsula Hotel, Salisbury Road, Kowloon; phone 366-6251) has been Hong Kong's see-and-be-seen café since the hotel—whose vast, Beaux Arts–ceilinged lobby it occupies in toto—went up in the 1920s. You may have simply a pot of tea or a prix-fixe scones-cum-tea. But if it were up to me, I would go all the way with the full tea—finger sandwiches, French pastries, scones with clotted cream and strawberry jam. Tea choices: Ceylon, Hediard's, Earl Grey, or Fortnum and Mason's Darjeeling. Fun. *First Class.*

Lobby Lounge (Conrad Hotel, Pacific Place, 88 Queensway, Hong Kong; phone 521-3838) is an ever-so-contemporary space—note the modern art on walls—that is as good a reason as any to experience this handsome hotel. Tea is traditional, its component parts (little sandwiches, scones, pastries) served from tiered silver trays. *First Class.*

Lobby Lounge (Regent Hotel, Salisbury Road, Kowloon; phone 721-1221): You no more miss a bout of tea in the dramatically high-ceilinged lobby lounge of the ever-so-mod Regent—with its high picture windows bringing the harbor and the Hong Kong skyline directly, it would seem, to your table—than you would an excursion to The Peak. The Regent serves up a set tea—sandwiches, scones, pastries—that's among the tastiest in town. Or you may choose à la carte. *First Class.*

AMERICAN

Beverly Hills Deli (Level 2, #55, New World Centre, Salisbury Road, east of the Regent Hotel, Kowloon; phone 369-8695) and 2 Lan Kwai Fong, near D'Aguilar Street, Central, Hong Kong; phone 801-5123): Beverly Hills *Deli*? No, I'm not kidding. If you're a big-city Yank who knows the genuine article, when it comes to corned beef, pastrami, salami, and the like, well, this is the genuine article exported to Hong Kong. Customary hours are 11 A.M. to 10 P.M., and the Deli delivers "to anywhere in Hong Kong." Just the thing when you may be a bit homesick. *First Class.*

Bostonian (Ramada Renaissance Hotel, 8 Peking Road, Kowloon; phone 311-3311) draws locals who want to pick a lobster from the tank for broiling or boiling, select their own steak for grilling, or choose a seafood special that's been flown in from Australia, New Zealand, Europe, or the U.S.—with American bluepoint oysters, cherrystone clams, and live Maine lobsters (from Boston) often available. There are other U.S. lures—U.S. Black Angus prime ribs, Cajun-style frog legs, pan fried sea bass, Caesar salad, and, among desserts, New York cheesecake, southern pecan pie, and Mom's apple pie—with a bit of bourbon in the vanilla ice cream plopped atop it. Good value buffet lunch, too. *First Class.*

Burger King and McDonald's, between them, constitute a minor Hong Kong phenomenon. There must be a couple score outlets, all told, packed with loquacious Chinese youths who tuck into Big Macs and Whoppers as though they had been weaned on them. If you want to sample the scene, the Burger King just opposite Star Ferry Terminal in Kowloon is as typical a locale as any. *Moderate.*

Central Park (15–16 Lan Kwai Fong, Central, Hong Kong; phone 845-4332): You like the look (not to mention the name, if you're from New York, as I am) of Central Park: so severely understated with its polished wood floors and immaculate white linen that it emerges as contemporarily elegant. There's a friendly feel to the place, and some notable American specialties. These include California chicken salad, Louisiana crab cakes and New England clam chowder among openers, grilled chicken breast, lamb chops, and sirloin steak (with all of which I suggest you ask for the sauces on the side—should they not be to your liking); and a generous sampling of California wines—including Robert Mondavi and Glen Ellen whites and reds. Desserts can be good: chocolate or strawberry soufflé, Häagen Dazs ice cream burying a warm apple tart, fruit crumble with custard sauce, chocolate brownies doused with whipped cream. With hot chocolate (a rarity in Hong Kong) among beverages, which include decaf cappuccino. *First Class.*

Harbourside (Regent Hotel, Salisbury Road; phone 721-1221): The world abounds in hotel coffee shops. None, I wager, is as beautiful as this one, down a level from the Regent lobby, so that its picture windows over the lobby are two stories high (views of the Hong Kong skyline are breathtaking and trees planted among the tables are indeed tall). There are, to be sure, non-American dishes on the menu. But those with stateside inspiration are so authentic and plentiful that I place Harbourside in this category. Openers include tomato cream soup, seafood chowder, panfried scallops, grilled shrimps, smoked salmon with sour cream. Your hot entrée might be filet of veal, sirloin steak, an omelet, or breast of chicken. There are other tempters: burgers, hot pastrami on rye, a steak sandwich or a hot dog, a tuna sandwich or turkey breast on toasted onion bread. Sweets? Ice cream sodas and milk shakes, sinful sundaes, strawberry fritters. And iced tea and iced coffee are always available. *First Class.*

ASIA BEYOND CHINA:
INDIA, JAPAN, OTHER LANDS

Benkay (Landmark Building, Pedder Street at Des Voeux Road, Central, Hong Kong; phone 521-3344) is, arguably, the quintessential Japanese restaurant, severely understated in look, in the best Japanese manner, with regular tables and *teppanyaki* counters for diners intent on a grilled-before-you Kobe steak or seafood specialty (shrimp are justifiably popular in this regard). Traditional dishes—tempura, for example—are on the menu, which is, however, crammed with what might be called, to us uninitiated, *nouvelle* Japanese—dishes you haven't known but which you might find pleasing. And worry not, sushi buffs, you'll be well taken care of. Consider, too, that there are prix-fixe menus at both midday and in the evening. Dressy. *First Class/ Luxury.*

Gaylord (Ashley Centre, 23 Ashley Road, Kowloon; phone 724-1001) is the Hong Kong outpost of a successful international network of Indian restaurants. Favorites are roasts from the tandoori oven—shrimp as well as chicken. Curries are good; ditto the kebabs. Note, too, the good-value lunchtime buffet. *First Class.*

Spices (Repulse Bay complex, Repulse Bay Road, Hong Kong; phone 812-2711; and in town at Shop 5–6, Mall, 1 Pacific Place, 88 Queensway, Hong Kong; phone 845-7978): The idea behind aptly named, appropriately exotic-looking Spices is to give the diner a delicious idea of non-Chinese

Asian cooking. The roundup of countries whose cuisines are represented reads like a Far Eastern UN: seafood salad from Indonesia, bamboo salad from Kampuchea (Cambodia), jellyfish salad from Vietnam—among cold appetizers, with warm options, too—including Singapore's spring rolls with pork and vegetables, Thailand's steamed seafood with red curry paste, India's *samosas*—deep-fried vegetable pastries and breads—*naan*, especially—are super. Entrées extend from, say Malaysia's deep-fried snapper with chili and tamarind juice to the Philippines' panfried squid and Korea's skewered beef tenderloin. Beer, generally, is the ideal beverage. Spices is different—and delightful. *First Class.*

Sui Sha Ya (440 Jaffe Road, Causeway Bay, Hong Kong; phone 838-1808, and also in Kowloon at 9 Chatham Road; phone 722-5001) is a Japanese class act, with both locations the epitome of subdued albeit splendid Japanese decor, backgrounds typically severe, and imported-from-Japan accents frequently as valuable as they are venerable. Clientele is largely execs—both from the country of origin and local—with decent expense accounts. Best buy—and, if you select the Causeway Bay outlet, nicely combined with a visit to the bay's Japanese department stores (Chapter 5). Emphasis is on seafood, *sashimi* for example, and, arguably the most popular specialty, broiled jumbo shrimp. The staff—with the women in gorgeous kimonos—is kind and efficient. If you're present for the all-inclusive lunch, *First Class*; otherwise, *Luxury*.

AUSTRIAN AND GERMAN

Baron's Table (Holiday Inn Golden Mile, 50 Nathan Road, Kowloon; phone 369-3111): A German restaurant in a Holiday Inn? It's authentic, attractive, and delicious, starting with the bread and rolls—quite as exemplary as in the country of origin, and good enough here to make a meal of. There's a prix-fixe lunch, but the à la carte is so extensive and so full of typical dishes I became fond of in researching *Germany at Its Best* that I suggest you peruse it; it's extensive but all dishes are translated from German into English. *Matjes* herring with two tasty sauces, suckling pig terrine in aspic, pea soup, and mushroom soup are openers to consider. There are veal and beef steaks, but you might want to opt for an entrée specialty—calf's liver Berlin-style (with apple slices, onions, and creamed potatoes), pickled pork knuckle in tandem with sauerkraut, and split-pea purée; braised beef *roulade* with red cabbage and my favorite meat dish in the German repertoire—*sauerbraten* (braised loin of beef) served with potato dumplings. German beers (which go well with German food) and German wines. And super sweets. *First Class.*

Mozart Stuben (8 Glenealy, Central, Hong Kong; phone 5221-1763): It was Gillian Stevens of the Hong Kong Hilton who first counseled Mozart Stuben; other Hong Kong residents recommended it, too, by the time I was able to book a table. This is a small spot (therein lies its charm) with a low table count. Owners Camilla and Ernst Ruckendorfer know their Austrian cuisine, prepare it deliciously, and serve it with a smile. *Mozartjause* (cold cuts and salami teamed with a snort of schnaps) is a favored opener, but so are duck liver terrine and horseradish-sauced smoked swordfish. Lentil soup afloat with bits of bacon and sliced sausage is a winner. Entrées present no problem: I tend to opt for *tafelspitz*—boiled beef with creamed spinach, sautéed potatoes, and apple horseradish; *Wienerschnitzel*, the veal masterwork served with salad and parsley potatoes; smoked pork loin; or—from neighboring Hungary—veal goulash with *Spätzle*-style noodles. If you're up to dessert, consider *Salzburg Nockerlin*—a kind of Austrian soufflé, with caramel and strawberry sauce; chocolate pancake with hazelnuts and cream; or *Wiener Eiskaffee*—iced coffee with vanilla ice cream. With your meal, order Austria's Gösser beer. *First Class.*

BREAKFAST

Breakfast in Hong Kong is quite as you like it. Hotels know both Western and Chinese dishes, and serve them with the kind of smile it's nice to have flashed, as you sit down for the first meal of the day. Invariably you may order à la carte or choose a club breakfast. And some of the top hotels— Mandarin Oriental, Peninsula, and Regent among them— have two breakfast venues. Withal, I want to call your attention to a single restaurant if you're not far from where it's located, or would like to make up a party.

Steak House (Regent Hotel, Salisbury Road, phone 721-1211): Don't let the name throw you. Lunch through dinner, this *is* just what the name implies (see below). But between 7 and 9:30 A.M. it serves up the meanest buffet breakfast east of Hawaii, where, in the course of researching and on a number of occasions re-researching *Hawaii at Its Best*, I became something of an expert on buffet breakfasts. That at the Steak House opens with assorted fresh fruits and juices, cereals and yogurts, cheese and cold cuts, and superb smoked salmon. You're ready, after openers, for a trip to the chef, where eggs or an omelet will be prepared as you indicate, served with ham, bacon, or sausages. Opt, if you like, for the Steak House's celebrated sirloin steak, breakfast-size, or whole-wheat pancakes. Your waiter will bring you bread, rolls, and coffee or tea, and at meal's end, back you go to the buffet for sweet pastries. Plan on a late lunch. *First Class.*

CHINESE

The Chinese restaurant in Hong Kong—simple noodle stands to palatial pavilions—is as common as the café in Paris. Because Chinese cuisine is one of the three great world foods—along with French and Italian—and because talented and enterprising Chinese have opened restaurants planet-wide, my assumption, with respect to readers of this book, is at least a certain familiarity with this cooking.

By and large—because most Hong Kong Chinese are of Cantonese origin—the province of Guandong, with its capital, Guangzhou (formerly Canton), is just over the frontier—Chinese cuisine is primarily of the Cantonese variety—among the finest. But there are restaurants, as well, with specialties of Beijing (still often called Peking for culinary purposes), Shanghai, Szechuan, and even Taiwan.

A few points:

1. There are many exceptions (a number called to your attention in pages following) but by and large, my conviction is that for the Western traveler, Chinese restaurants in good hotels—invariably attractive, with staffs that smile and speak fairly good if not necessarily fluent English, appealing table appointments, and unpatronizing attitudes toward Westerners—are the best bet for us.

2. Whether you use them at home in Chinese restaurants or not, in Hong Kong—at least in my not inconsiderable experience, Westerner or not—you will be provided with chopsticks (and the curved porcelain spoons used for liquids) rather than knives and forks. I offer a simple technique for chopstick use in Chapter 1. You will learn quickly and, believe me, easily, by trying (ideally at a Chinese restaurant or two at home before departing for Hong Kong) and by watching fellow diners. One point I will make: the little bowls in which rice is served are lifted directly to the mouth with one hand, while the other transfers rice with the aid of chopsticks directly into the mouth. (Breakfast is

Western-style with Western cutlery, and you may, in most places request Western cutlery at lunch and dinner.)

3. If there are Chinese members of your party in a restaurant, particularly one not in a better hotel—you'll find, invariably, that the waiting staff will speak Chinese to your Chinese friends and ignore you, as though you might be a small child out with Mommy and Daddy for the first time. On the other hand, enter a Chinese restaurant without Chinese friends, and more often than not, English-speaking staffers will take good care of you.

4. Of course, let captains and waiters make suggestions from the menu. But stand by your own concept of what might appeal. If, for example, you've trekked through the public market of a morning (Chapter 5) and seen live snakes by the bushel-basketful, many being skinned by owners as you pass by, you may not want to try snake soup, even if it's suggested. Simply smile and order something that sounds more to your taste.

5. *Dim sum*, if you haven't tried it at home, is the catchall phrase for bite-size goodies, consumed with tea, and often the basis, in Chinese restaurants both in Hong Kong and China as well as countries abroad, including the U.S., of a tasty lunch. You make selections from bamboo baskets that are wheeled past you on trolleys. Chinese-speaking customers often place *dim sum* orders by checking off what they want on small *dim sum* order blanks. On such occasions, you'll need help. *Dim sum*, paid for by the piece, are usually served through mid-afternoon; three or four is the usual quantity ordered.

6. Invariably, you're greeted with a hot towel for your hands and, if you wish, your face, at the beginning and end of each meal, with tea an automatic starting beverage. Some restaurants bring several small plates of often unappetizing little nibbles with tea—for which you're charged even though you haven't ordered them, unless you attempt sending them back—not always easy.

7. A word about bird's nest, shark's fin, Chinese teas, and Chinese wines. Bird's nest soup is tastier than the title implies: its base is the nest-building congealed saliva of cliff-dwelling swallows, carefully cleaned and prepared, and sometimes appearing sweetened by sugar, as a dessert. Shark's fin is the genuine article—dried fin cartilages that are used in soups, and often graded for quality, as is, for example, beef in the United States. Tea—a Chinese staple since before Jesus Christ was born—is believed to aid digestion and clear the palate. As I indicate above, it's served upon arrival in restaurants, without being ordered, but is sometimes charged for, albeit minimally; it's drunk without sugar or milk in smallish cups, sometimes with lids. (You'll notice that workers in offices, shops, and factories have their own covered teacups—much larger than those used in restaurants.) Tea comes green (unfermented), oolong (partially fermented), and black (highly fermented). Jasmine is probably the most popular. Chinese wines are not really wines but rather spirits distilled from rice millet, herbs, and sometimes even flowers. The most appropriate with meals is dry sherrylike Siu Hang. Most people, however, prefer tea, beer, or Western dry white wines with Chinese foods, unless it's very rich like, say, Peking duck, when a stout red is indicated.

Eagle's Nest (Hong Kong Hilton Hotel, 2 Queen's Road, Central, Hong Kong; phone 523-3311), what with its dramatic rooftop situation and smashing views from its windows, is quite the most strikingly situated Chinese restaurant in town. And surely one of its most delicious. Specialties are both Cantonese and northern Chinese, and in the evening there's dancing to an orchestra, if you please. Not your everyday Chinese restaurant, to be sure. *Dim sum* in the form of a variety of dumplings, barbecued pork, and sweet bean curd, to name some, is a favorite midday. But the menu runs a broad gamut—braised snake soup and sautéed duck, barbecued duck or pork, steamed lion fish and steamed pork, deep fried bean curd with minced pork sauce and crabmeat and rice noodles in a clay pot—to give you an idea. *First Class/Luxury.*

East Ocean (Harbour Centre, 25 Harbour Road, Wan Chai, Hong Kong Island; phone 893-8887) is as good a reason as any for an excursion out on the island. This is a popular spot, so you must reserve in advance, concentrating on seafood specialties and surprisingly good sweets, including macadamia nut puffs. *First Class.*

Fook Lam Moon (31 Mody Road, Kowloon; phone 366-0286, and 35–45 Johnston Road, Wanchai, Hong Kong; phone 866-0663) draws infinitely more Chinese than foreign customers. The food is okay but service, in my experience, can be so painfully slow as to spoil a meal. Consider such dishes as sautéed shrimp with walnuts, half a baked chicken deliciously sauced, sliced beef with vegetables and Cantonese hot pot. But only if you have unlimited time—and patience. *First Class.*

Golden Leaf (Conrad Hotel, Pacific Place, 88 Queensway, Hong Kong; phone 521-3838) wows first-timers before they've eaten a morsel. This is a spectacular space with gilded doors from four dynasties (Ming, Tang, Yuan, and Ching) and perfectly delicious things to eat. You make your choice from one of the most extensive Chinese menus in town—braised noodles with sliced lobster in bouillon, sautéed minced shrimp with water chestnuts, poached cabbage with ham, deep fried prawn balls with crabmeat. Or how about barbecued sliced eel, baked spareribs, sweet and sour pork, roasted chicken with chicken liver and Yunnan ham? Lovely service. *First Class/Luxury.*

Guangzhou Garden (Exchange Square, Central, Hong Kong; phone 525-1163) affords beautiful views of the harbor and Kowloon from picture windows, and is among the more subtly decorated of the Chinese restaurants in Hong Kong. Not that fare takes second place. Specialties include shark's fin and bird's nest soup. You may or may not be courageous enough to order double-boiled snake. But there's so much else: grilled king prawns, sautéed scallops, chicken with ham in a basket, roasts of goose and duck, barbecued suckling pig. Everything that I've tasted is delicious. *First Class/Luxury.*

Heichinrou (Sun Plaza, 28 Canton Road, Kowloon; phone 721-7123) stuns with a decor melding black walls with red accents—including carnations of the latter color on tables and black-accented staff uniforms. It's a pleasure to make a lunch of *dim sum* here, but you may have a proper meal, perhaps basing it on deservedly popular roast chicken. *First Class/Luxury.*

Hei Fung Terrace (Repulse Bay Road, Repulse Bay; phone 812-2622) embraces a quite marvelous mix of wood ceiling beams, Chinese lanterns, elaborate woodwork, and reproductions of antique Chinese chairs at tables, the lot set off by stark white linen. Specialties are Pekinese and Szechuanese. They run to chicken, abalone, and shrimp soups, braised seafood with chili and sour sauce served in a hot pot, and sautéed scallops and shrimps with peppers. *First Class/Luxury.*

Hunan Garden (Forum, Exchange Square, Hong Kong; phone 868-2880) conveniently indicates its really hot Hunan specialties with two printed pepper pods on the menu, with the moderately hot accorded only one, and the non-hot, none. I like to go all the way with such extra-hots as fried prawns with chili and fried chicken. But there are more moderately hot choices, cuttlefish with peppers and spring onion sauce and sautéed scallops among them. Special. *First Class.*

Jumbo Floating Restaurant (Aberdeen, Hong Kong Island; phone 873-7111): Presumably a Westerner's concept of what China and Chinese decor are all about, this grossly gaudy, permanently moored, multilevel vessel in Aberdeen harbor has been packing in visitors—groups especially—for as long as I have known Hong Kong. If it is not taken seriously by Hong Kong residents, visitors compensate—and in droves. You may—or may not—want to bother with this excursion from town; fare is Cantonese—crabmeat soup and boiled shrimp, chicken with cashews, and what else if not fried rice? *First Class.*

Lai Ching Heen (Regent Hotel, Salisbury Road, Kowloon; phone 721-1211): In a city with more than its share of attractive Chinese restaurants, Lai Ching Heen—with picture windows giving onto the harbor, exquisite jade table settings, with rose and pale gray the dominant colors—emerges, at least in my experience, as the most beautiful. The menu, at both lunch and dinner, is à la carte and extensive, but with a relatively abbreviated selection of chef's specialties on its last page. Consider spicy dumplings with cabbage, noodles with ginger and scallions in abalone sauce, pork and pineapple rolls, and such other standouts as roast duck with jellyfish, sautéed sliced beef and bamboo shoots, deep-fried chicken with Yunnan ham, fresh lobster and poached shrimp, roast pigeon, and the chef's special scallops. If you're going to splurge for one top-category Chinese restaurant, I would suggest Lai Ching Heen. *Luxury.*

Luk Kwok Hotel (72 Gloucester Road, Wanchai, Hong Kong; phone 866-2166) calls its restaurant the Canton

Room, but customers mostly use the name of the hotel to identify the eatery. You may order any of three multicourse prix-fixe menus—for which a gargantuan appetite is indicated. Or from the Chinese-language à la carte, from which the captain translates and invariably comes up with corking good suggestions, as, for example, a dinner that might include sautéed scallops in a ham sauce, a platter of shrimp prepared in two styles, roast pigeon Mongol-style, and roast chicken Canton-style. With such other options as shark's fin soup and roast suckling pig. *First Class/Luxury.*

Loong Yuen (Holiday Inn Golden Mile Hotel, 50 Nathan Road, Kowloon; phone 739-6268)—in a setting of ivory and peach brocaded walls and upholstery—makes a specialty of Cantonese seafood, and is justifiably proud of such dishes as lobster with shrimps, crab, and scallops. Braised winter melon with mushrooms is delicious, too. *First Class.*

Man Ho (J. W. Marriott Hotel, Pacific Place, 88 Queensway, Hong Kong; phone 810-8366) is easily in the top rung of Hong Kong's Chinese restaurants. Barbecue platters are a specialty of note—of pork, goose, chicken, or a combination thereof, with roast suckling pig exemplary, too. Seafood dishes are special—baked stuffed crab, lobster baked in the shell, sautéed shrimp balls with garlic, to name some tempters. Roasted crispy chicken always has takers. Ditto spareribs and fried noodles with shredded beef. *First Class/Luxury.*

Ma Wah (Mandarin Oriental Hotel, 5 Connaught Road, Central, Hong Kong; phone 522-0111): You start here with setting. Floor is the 25th, walls are punctuated with picture windows, views of harbor and city are extraordinary, and traditionally designed rosewood chairs flank tables, beneath a network of brass lanterns. The menu opens with cold platters—never favorites of mine in the Chinese cuisine. Better one of the soups—shark's fin, bird's nest, corn-and-crabmeat. Ma Wah's seafood is superior—garlic-sauced lobster; scallop and prawn hot pot; deep-fried crab-meat roll. This is an ideal spot for Peking duck and for spareribs. And it's among the relatively few Chinese restaurants with a decent-sized dessert card—including unusual lotus-seed pancakes, mango pudding, and sweetened almond cream with honey. *Luxury.*

Peking Garden (Alexandra House, Central, Hong Kong, and also at Excelsior Shopping Mall, Causeway Bay, Hong Kong; phones, respectively, 526-6456, 577-7231): Your primary mission at Peking Garden is the placement of an order for Peking duck. Scallop and shrimp dishes are good, too. Unless the Causeway Bay branch has had a facelift of late, the in-town Peking Garden is the more attractive of the pair. *First Class.*

Pine & Bamboo (103 Sai Yeung Choi Street, Kowloon, and 3 Leighton Road, Hong Kong; phones 394-7195 and 577-4914, respectively) is indicated for excellent specialties—Peking duck, beggar's chicken (which must be ordered a day in advance, but it's worth the bother), and a fabulous Mongolian hot pot. *First Class.*

Prince Court (Shop 115, Ocean Galleries, Harbour City, 21 Canton Road, Kowloon; phone 730-8939) is a delightful source of hot and spicy Szechuan cuisine, which in recent years has become popular in the United States. Shrimp dishes are standouts—shrimp balls with chili sauce, fried shrimp, shrimp in hot garlic sauce. Poultry tempts, too; spicy chicken, for example. Sliced pork Szechuan-style is a winner; ditto filet of beef with dry chili. Friendly. *First Class.*

Regal Seafood Restaurant (Regal Meridien Hotel, 71 Mody Road, Kowloon; phone 722-1818) may not sound Chinese, but is it ever—and not only for seafood at that. The menu goes on for pages, but you can do very well ordering from the limited segment called Special Suggestions, the range seafood soup, stewed chicken with fungus and lily flowers (yes, lily flowers—but don't be afraid), sautéed chicken wings in chili sauce, and stewed crabs with vermicelli in satay sauce. With an exceptional range of noodle dishes. *First Class.*

Shang Palace (Kowloon Shangri-La Hotel, 64 Mody Road, Kowloon; phone 721-2111) is nothing if not spiffy, what with framed scrolls on red lacquer walls, traditional Chinese ceiling lanterns, in a setting that's architecturally clean-lined and contemporary. Go midday for either of two prix-fixe lunches. You might open with black mushroom soup and choose from two main dishes—combination barbecue and panfried sliced chicken, for example. Cordial service. *First Class.*

Spring Moon (Peninsula Hotel, Salisbury Road, Kowloon; phone 739-2332) is indicated at midday, when you tuck into the prix-fixe *dim sum* menu—opening with a combination plate, continuing with diced seafood and bean curd soup, preparatory to a fish fillet, itself in advance of sautéed sliced beef with noodle soup following (in the Chinese fashion), and petits fours presented at meal's end, with chilled mango pudding. Setting is a handsome room that's a study in pale gray. *Luxury.*

Tai Woo (17 Wellington Street, Central, Hong Kong; phone 524-5618) is at its liveliest midday, when workers in the neighborhood flock in for the prix-fixe lunch or order seafood à la carte. Odd as it may sound, consider scrambled creamy crabmeat—or if you would rather, one of the chicken dishes. *First Class.*

FRENCH

When French cuisine leaves France, it can remain completely authentic, or it can take on variations, be they contemporary versions of traditional dishes, regional/local variations on Gallic themes, or even creative new dishes, the work of talented chefs. In the case of Hong Kong, where the Chinese cooking—one of the three great world cuisines, along with French and Italian—dominates, expect a change here or a variation there, in the course of menu perusal. On the other hand, there are a number of determinedly French eateries. I provide a sampling of each type herewith. In my experience, their range is, by and large, corking good to exceptional.

Café de Paris (30 D'Aigular Street, Central, Hong Kong; phone 524-7521) is the very personal bailiwick of French-born—and to this day decidedly French—Maurice Gardette. Indeed, on his business card, he makes the following statement loud and clear:

French Traditional Cuisine
French Atmosphere
French Owner
French Chef
Très Très
French

Okay, now you have it. Monsieur Gardette's best value is prix-fixe lunch, but in the evening or at any time the à la carte features specialties like *foie gras, pâté de campagne, bœuf marchand du vin* with luxurious truffles an occasional garnish. Accompany your meal with wine. The entire cellar is

French. If you're a confirmed Francophile like me, you'll like Café de Paris. *First Class.*

Trou Normand (6 Carnarvon Road, Kowloon; phone 366-8754) is an only-in-Hong Kong kind of French restaurant. By that I mean it's now (if not originally) Chinese-owned and -staffed, chefs included. But the menu remains traditionally French, service is delightful, and everything that I've ordered is tasty. Coarse country-style pâté is a good opener, as are also *escargots de Bourgogne*, Norwegian smoked salmon, and a nifty *salade Niçoise*. Filet of sole is prepared with a rich sauce as in Normandy, but you may have it simply grilled. Favorites like *coq au vin, steak au poivre,* and tournedos served with a not-bad béarnaise sauce are good bets, too. Desserts include *crêpes Suzette,* not all that frequently come across contemporarily, and bananas flamed with rum. French wines. *First Class.*

Gaddi's (Peninsula Hotel, Salisbury Road; phone 366-6251) retains its longtime title as Hong Kong's glamour queen. Its look—in soft tones, capacious and elegant of ambience—is its first plus. Its service—the staff, maître d', captains, waiters, buspersons—is congenial and competent, albeit never obtrusive. Which leaves fare: everything I've tasted is delicious. There's a prix-fixe at both lunch and dinner, comprising two courses and coffee served with petits fours. But the à la carte is outstanding enough for you to consider instead. Hors d'oeuvres range extends from Beluga caviar and smoked Scotch salmon through *pistou*-sauced snails and crabmeat-filled crêpes, with lobster bisque a standout among soups. Poached sea bass and smoked salmon are popular fish choices, and if you're going to try pigeon—very popular in Hong Kong—Gaddi's is the place to do so. Beef is superb with respect to quality and preparation—*entrecôte* especially. But there are veal and lamb specialties, too. And you don't want to skip *pommes soufflés.* If enough of your red dinner wine remains, cheese is a wise concluding course, but sweets are super, too: chocolate and hazelnut soufflé, Amaretto-sauced, for example. *Luxury.*

La Brasserie (Regal Meridien Hotel, 71 Mody Road, Kowloon; phone 722-1818): Though it is more casual than the Regal Meridien's Restaurant de France (below), La Brasserie is quite as French. Tempting openers include smoked goose with leeks and mushrooms, duck mousse, snails Burgundy-style, a delicious *gratin* of endive teamed with ham, and onion soup. Linguini is a super entrée, as indeed is roast duck, and you want to conclude with this house's esteemed apple tart. There are good-value prix-fixe menus at both lunch and dinner. *First Class.*

Le Must (33 D'Aguilar Street, Central, Hong Kong; phone 521-4211) is good-looking, good-tasting, attractively populated, and with a friendly staff. Best bet is the set lunch, which might open with the day's soup, avocado and papaya salad, or ravioli; with panfried fish interestingly sauced, and calf's liver typical entrées; desserts as well. The à la carte is more expensive, always with unusual, albeit delicious soups, seafood entrées like scallops with lobster sauce, lamb chops, and filet of beef. To conclude: the good cheese board or a tasty lemon tart. *First Class.*

Pierrot (Mandarin Oriental Hotel, 5 Connaught Road, Hong Kong; phone 522-0111)—among the grander of the French restaurants—affords spectacular views—it's on the 25th floor—and offers authentic cuisine of France. Best time to go is on a clear day at lunchtime, the better for the vistas, and for the three-course prix-fixe, which might open with an unusual rabbit-cauliflower salad with a mustard-accented vinaigrette and the day's soup or pasta as options. Follow with an entrée like Scotch salmon, roast veal, or breast of chicken—creatively prepared and sauced; and wind up with imported French cheeses from a generous-sized board, ice cream, or pastry. The set meal is available at dinner, too, but at that hour you might want to sample the à la carte, opening perhaps with *carpaccio* of Welsh lamb, thyme-flavored in olive vinaigrette, teamed with artichoke mousse or lobster consommé, continuing with salmon and scallops, venison *medaillons*, or Provençal-style roast lamb. If you can manage a sweet, make it mint parfait with strawberries in tandem with chocolate and rum-cream sauce. Fine French wines. *Luxury.*

Restaurant de France (Regal Meridien Hotel, 71 Mody Road, Kowloon; phone 722-1818)—a leader among Hong Kong's French restaurants—occupies a turn-of-century-style room, with half a dozen stained-glass ceiling domes out of France its decorative highlight. Fare is fairly standard Gallic—and top rank, with snails, scallops, and seafood terrine among openers; a rich cream of leek soup, mussel-studded; leek-wrapped shrimp with bacon; and—possibly the restaurant's most noted specialty—roast duck (for two). Breast of pheasant and rack of lamb are good entrées, too. For dessert, I counsel coffee and rum-flavored pastry, filled with chocolate mousse. Pleasant service. *Luxury.*

Le Tire Bouchon (9 Old Bailey Street, Central, Hong Kong; phone 523-5459) is, to be sure, unpretentious, but the grub's good—snails and *foie gras* among openers, lamb and pork specialties, not easily come by seafood dishes, and France's justly celebrated upside-down cake—*Tarte Tatin*, ever-reliable for dessert. French wines. *First Class.*

Lalique (Royal Garden Hotel, Mody Road, Kowloon; phone 721-5215) Lalique? As in the French sculpted glass by that name? Is it ever. Lalique is the basis of the decor. Besides temptingly tabbed prix-fixe lunches and dinners, there's a dilly of an à la carte. House-made *foie gras de canard*, lobster salad, caviar and lobster bisque are among first courses. Grilled sea bass is a fish favorite; smoked duck, lamb chops, and filet of beef are popular entrées, too, the latter especially good with the chef's sauce béarnaise. Rich sweets and worthy wines. *Luxury.*

Plume (Regent Hotel, Salisbury Road, Kowloon; phone 721-1211) is the premier restaurant of a premier hotel. Reserve your table adjacent to picture windows on either of two levels, and you'll enjoy the harbor view as much as your meal, in a room embellished with Oriental works of art, with 14-carat-gold-bordered porcelain and hand-blown Bavarian glassware on tables. The house starts you off with a complimentary glass of champagne-myr, the myr signifying a dash of blueberry liqueur, along with that marvelous Indian bread, *naan*, and goose liver-green peppercorn *pâté*. From then on, your meal is up to you. My most recent Plume dinner (the restaurant is not open for lunch) was a prix-fixe that began with *carpaccio* of marinated sea bass in shallot-herb vinaigrette. It was followed by tomato consommé, chicken-and-vegetable embellished. Salmon and scallop charlotte was the fish course, preparatory to fillet of lamb in potato truffle crust—one of Hong Kong's great dishes. Almond chocolate pudding on vanilla sauce was the sweet, and petits fours accompanied coffee. The à la carte offers considerable choices—smoked quail, lobster salad, artichoke soup topped with a dollop of caviar, and venison consommé among first courses; grilled and smoked sea bass with caviar sauce and braised salmon in a horseradish crust among the fish; prime beef, roast veal, and lamb fillet among entrées. Desserts can be sublime, and the cellar has 8,000 bottles of wine (guests are welcome to have a look, with the sommelier), including selections from California and rare vintages from auctions at Christie's and Sotheby's in London. Indeed, wine buffs find the list worth keeping. A special place. *Luxury.*

Stanley's French Restaurant (86 Stanley Main Street, Stanley, Hong Kong Island; phone 813-8873) is worth knowing about for a midday pause if you've spent the morning at Stanley Market or are about to spend the afternoon. The prix-fixe might run to pea soup, ribs of beef, a frozen sweet, and coffee, served with cookies. *Moderate/First Class.*

INTERNATIONAL

Ambassador Hotel Coffee Shop (26 Nathan Road, Kowloon; phone 366-6321) is worth noting because of the diversity of its menu—the range smoked salmon or Burgundy-style snails as starters, club sandwiches and burgers, *wonton* and other Chinese soups and entrées, omelets through steaks. *Moderate.*

Fountainside (Landmark Building lobby, Central, Hong Kong) is a watch-the-world-go-by café in one of the busiest—and smartest—settings in town. A nice stop for midmorning coffee, afternoon tea, or if you're flush, lunch. *Luxury.*

Maxim's Express (Railway Station, Kowloon) is brought to your attention only because, in the course of waiting for a train—to China, perhaps—you may require sustenance. This is a so-so and, in my opinion, overpriced cafeteria, with an attached waitress-service restaurant. *Moderate.*

Gripps (Omni Hong Kong Hotel, 3 Canton Road, Harbour City, Kowloon; phone 736-0088) is inviting and with respect to its fare, a happy mix from, say, mussel salad, pigeon terrine, sautéed scampi, and lobster chowder among openers through a first-rate *salade Niçoise* (a good choice at lunch) and sandwiches such as Black Forest ham on dark German bread, smoked salmon on pumpernickel, and a mean club, served on toasted brioche. Satisfying seafood and poultry, too. Apple-filled pancake flamed with Calvados is among snappy sweets. *First Class.*

The Grill (Hong Kong Hilton Hotel, 2 Queen's Road, Central, Hong Kong; phone 523-3111) is at its most amusing midday—busy and bustling with business and professional neighbors mixed with hotel visitors. The name of the game is contemporary cuisine—bluefin tuna *carpaccio*, truffled duck-liver salad, roast grouse among appetizers, crab bisque and thyme-scented mussel soup, roast salmon and grilled turbot, a whole roast pheasant, charred beef tenderloin, and roast American prime rib, carved at your table. If you're up to dessert, make it hot hazelnut prune terrine with poppyseed ice cream—and think of me while you're enjoying it. Super service. *Luxury.*

J.K.'s on the Peak (100 Peak Road, Victoria Peak, Hong Kong; phone 848-7788) is popular with Hong Kong residents, who like its good looks, the professional service, and the grilled specialties—steak, chops, poultry especially, with hearty soups among openers, and an interesting wine list. *First Class.*

J.W.'s Grill (J.W. Marriott Hotel, Pacific Place, 88 Queensway, Central, Hong Kong; phone 810-8366) hits the spot when you're hungry for a meal reminiscent of home. There are prix-fixe lunches and dinners—excellent value to be sure. But the à la carte tempts, as for example prosciutto ham teamed with melon, Caesar salad, and lobster bisque among openers; salmon steak and fried red snapper, half a dozen species of beefsteak, sirloin and T-bone among them, breast of chicken, loin of baby lamb, and—best for last—prime rib of U.S. beef. Desserts are limited in variety but are winners, bitter chocolate cake especially. Exemplary cellar. Lovely service. *Luxury*.

Mandarin Grill (Mandarin Oriental Hotel, 5 Connaught Road, Central, Hong Kong; phone 522-0111) is smartly split-level, with mural-surfaced walls, comfy armchairs at tables, and an extensive à la carte. Start with smoked salmon or Italian-inspired *antipasti*, charred tuna on lentil salad, mixed hors d'oeuvres, fried crab cakes, or the grill's crab and pumpkin soup. Call for the silver wagon to be rolled tableside the while American Black Angus prime rib is served you. There are half a dozen types of steak, Dutch and Welsh lamb, and poultry from France. Or select a lobster from the tank, prepared as you direct. Desserts are spectacular, wines top of the line. *Luxury*.

Peak Café (121 Peak Road, Victoria Peak, Hong Kong) is nice to drop in at any time of day, breakfast through dinner. If you arrive midday, there's a good-value prix-fixe lunch, which might include one of the house's inventive salads, choice of entrées (Indian curries are good here), and fresh fruit cocktail topped with ice cream. Soups, sandwiches, afternoon tea, too. *Moderate*.

Peak Tower Coffee Shop (Victoria Peak, Hong Kong; phone 849-7260)—the lower down and less pricey of a pair of Peak Tower eateries, both with extraordinary views of Hong Kong below—is one of a pair of Peak eateries operated by the Peninsula Hotel (the other is the Peak Tower Restaurant, below). The coffee shop is ideal for a midmorning pick-me-up or for lunch, with good sandwiches, burgers, and salads, standard Western and Chinese entrées, desserts and drinks, alcoholic and otherwise, and buffet breakfast Sundays and holidays, usually between 8 A.M. and 10 A.M. *Moderate.*

Peak Tower Restaurant (Victoria Peak, Hong Kong; phone 849-7260) is a wise lunch choice—you select all you like from a buffet. Dinner is served daily, traditionally until as late as 11:30 P.M. from an à la carte that might open with crab meat and shrimp, or *strudel*-wrapped goose liver, featuring U.S. imported steaks, and whole Dover sole among entrées, with poached pear in red wine among desserts. On weekends and holidays, pause for afternoon tea. *First Class.*

Peninsula Hotel Lobby (Salisbury Road, Kowloon; phone 366-6251) is Hong Kong's favorite congregating spot, breakfast through dinner, including coffee in the morning, tea in the afternoon, and drinks in the evening. Customers are surprised at the extensive à la carte, smoked salmon and beef *tartar*, onion and barley soups, *salade Niçoise* and eggs Benedict, club and Reuben among the sandwiches, pizza and *dim sum*, ravioli and beef stew, with a range of sweets as well as prix-fixe lunches and dinners. First Hong Kong visit or fifteenth, nobody omits a pilgrimage to the Peninsula Lobby. *First Class/Luxury.*

Verandah Restaurant (Repulse Bay, Hong Kong; phone 812-2722): If you've been a Hong Kong visitor over the years, you'll no doubt remember the lovely Repulse Bay Hotel out on the island. What happened, in recent seasons, is that a graceless apartment house was built atop its base. Fortunately, the remaining lower portion remains the site of several restaurants, Verandah the best known and most visited. If it's warm and sunny, take a terrace table, and order a lunch that might open with grilled scallops, sautéed goose liver, or French onion soup, preparatory to, say, flamed prawns with shellfish in an herb sauce, sirloin steak, or Caesar salad. Hot soufflés are a dessert specialty. Wines—Australian, California, Spanish, Italian, German, Swiss, the various French regions—are in abundance and well priced. A smart bar is adjacent; it's nice for a pre-meal aperitif. *First Class/Luxury.*

Window Café, Kowloon Hotel (19 Nathan Road, Kowloon; phone 369-8698) rates an A for its specialties—smoked salmon out of Norway on toasted rye; Parma ham on Italian bread with mozzarella; British afternoon tea sandwiches, finger-style; shrimp, tuna, and egg salads; Provençale mushrooms and ham; Indonesian chicken satay with peanut sauce; UK scones with cream and jam. *Moderate.*

ITALIAN

Capriccio (Ramada Renaissance Hotel, 8 Peking Road, Kowloon; phone 311-3311) boasts one of the most extensive Italian menus in Hong Kong. It's not easy to choose from the à la carte—mixed *antipasto* or artichoke salad, mussel or minestrone soup, and utterly delicious pastas— *tortellini ai quatro formaggio, fettuccini ai porcine e tartufo bianco, paglia e fieno, linguine ai ragu di vongole*—among pastas, with half a dozen each fish and meat entrées, including grilled fresh seafood with garlic, oil, and lemon, and *osso bucco.* Buffet lunch—never with less than nine pastas, ten fish and meat entrées, and a choice of five desserts plus coffee—is excellent value. *First Class.*

Espresso (Hong Kong Hilton Hotel, 2 Queen's Road, Central, Hong Kong; phone 523-3111): Hilton International, with several hotels in Italy, knows that country's cuisine, as you soon appreciate at Espresso. Open with *calamari fritti* (deep-fried squid in tomato sauce), minestrone or tomato soup, Caesar or eggplant and artichoke salad. I wish that there were more than four pastas, but those I've had—including lasagna as well as *risotto con quatro formaggi*—have been excellent. There are pizzas, too, and Florentine-style steak, *osso bucco*, and Tuscan-style braised chicken among entrées. A platter of Italian cheese ideally concludes a meal. Friendly. *First Class.*

Grissini (Grand Hyatt Hotel, 1 Harbour Road, Wanchai, Hong Kong; phone 861-1234): What better name for an Italian restaurant than the term for Italy's celebrated bread-sticks? Grissini is stylish and contemporary. But you go for the fare, prepared under the supervision of an imported-from-Milan chef, with an extensive menu, the range arugula and tomato salad, a platter of assorted salamis, or the classic *vitello tonnato* out of Piedmont among openers. Fettucini, cappellini, rigatoni, lasagna, and risotto are memorable, too. Seafood (garlicky fried shrimp, for example) and roast chicken entrées are successful, too, and authentic *zuppa inglese* is among sweets. Italian wines. *Luxury.*

Nicholini's (Conrad Hotel, Pacific Place, 88 Queensway, Hong Kong; phone 521-3838) is arguably the handsomest of Hong Kong's Italian restaurants—floral-upholstered banquettes complement floral carpet, set against green upholstered chairs, and wall murals are striking—but it's also very tasty. This is the only Italian restaurant in Hong Kong where I've come across the appetizer called *bresaola*—seasoned dried beef—here served with mushroom and celery salad. Assorted *antipasti* are satisfying, as indeed are snails in pesto sauce with bacon and mushrooms, and that old standby soup, *pasta e fagioli*. I particularly like Nicholini's because of its broad choice of pasta—taglioline and capelli, linguini and ravioli, cannelloni and farfalle, pennette and spaghetti. Those that I've had are delicious; ditto *osso bucco* and *scallopini di vitello* from among entrées.

Desserts are traditional—including *tiramisù, zabaglione,* and *cassata Siciliana.* Italian wines. *Luxury.*

Pizzeria (Kowloon Hotel, 19 Nathan Road, Kowloon; phone 369-8698) is deceptively named in that it is a full Italian restaurant, serving a lot more than pizza. And a standout restaurant at that. Open with *crespelle,* stuffed Tuscan pancakes, *lasagna verdi, polenta* with Parma ham and Gorgonzola cheese, or minestrone afloat with the stuffed pasta squares called tortellini. There are close to an additional dozen pastas, and Italian entrées based on shrimp and veal, lamb and chicken, with beefsteaks, too. Italian wines. *First Class.*

Valentino Hanoi Road (16 Hanoi Road, Kowloon; phone 721-6349): Poor service is a rarity, praise be, in Hong Kong. But at this ordinary-looking eatery my party and I exited for another restaurant, after an excessive wait for a waiter. I can't recommend Valentino's. *First Class.*

STEAKS

Louis' Steak House (50 Gloucester Road, Hong Kong; phone 529-8933): Louis' primary asset, so far as I can perceive, is size; it's big. The decor, though, is undistinguished; ditto the steaks I've sampled. I can't recommend this one. *First Class.*

Steak House (Regent Hotel, Salisbury Road, Kowloon; phone 721-1211): The look is Windsor chairs and framed antique prints, tall plants and picture-window views of the harbor. And the fare relates almost exclusively to what the name implies: steaks—choose sirloin, rib-eye, T-bone, or filet mignon (most come in two sizes) with such options as lamb chops, veal, or chicken, not to mention fresh lobster and fresh salmon. You open with a salad of your own composition from the giant salad bar. All entrées are charcoal-broiled and served with baked Idaho potato, onion rings, and cherry tomatoes. And the staff is alert and cheerful. *Luxury.*

SUNDAY BRUNCH

Banyan Grill (Conrad Hotel, Pacific Place, 88 Queensway, Hong Kong; phone 521-3938): Hey! It's just like home: eggs Benedict and smoked salmon, French toast and sirloin steak, hash browns and corned beef hash, waffles and pancakes, bagels and Danish—with all the coffee you like, and the Sunday papers. Hours subject of course to change, are 11 A.M. to 3 P.M. *First Class.*

SWISS

Chesa (Peninsula Hotel, Salisbury Road, Kowloon; phone 366-6251): I haven't been to a restaurant outside Switzerland since researching *Switzerland at Its Best* that's as authentically and deliciously Swiss as this one. There's a good-value prix-fixe lunch that's popular with business regulars, but I suggest opting for the à la carte, chockablock with Swiss specialties from, say, dried paper-thin Swiss ham, sliced Swiss-style sausage, snails braised in Swiss white wine, spinach dumplings, and Swiss barley cream soup with air-dried beef among openers. There are fish entrées but those in the meat section remind one more of the country of origin; I refer to Zürich-style veal with mushrooms in a light cream sauce, Swiss sausage with onion sauce, leek and potato casserole, and *plat du conseiller*—assorted broiled meats in tandem with Switzerland's marvelous *rösti* potatoes, these last served with all entrées, for which three cheers. *Luxury.*

5

Hong Kong to Buy

SETTING THE SHOPPING SCENE

As a foot-weary inspector—in the line of duty—of shops of every category in the world's major cities (and many minor ones, as well), I can say without exaggeration that the shopping scene in Hong Kong is like no other.

It was, when I started visiting Hong Kong, not a few seasons back, relatively sane and simple and invariably good value. Your goals were primarily custom-made clothing and Oriental objets d'art. Gradually, as neighboring China began to trade internationally (if not yet to welcome foreign visitors), Chinese-made merchandise found its way to Hong Kong—crafts and textiles and all manner of bibelots.

Not long thereafter, the Chinese opened craft stores of their own—they constitute a major chain in Hong Kong —and almost simultaneously foreign firms (mostly American) began to employ cheap Hong Kong labor to manufacture clothing according to U.S. designers' specifications. And, ere long, the occasional factory-outlet shop—for irregulars, seconds, and discontinued models of garments —attracted shoppers with good reason: bargain prices.

As tourism became a major Hong Kong industry, the number of Hong Kong residents increased; the territory found itself flooded with people (population density is among the world's highest) and shops for them to spend their money, not only in the two principal visitor areas—Kowloon and Hong Kong Central—but island-wide.

Everything was hunky-dory, for the American shopper at least, so long as the dollar remained strong. But as the eighties became the nineties, the dollar weakened, the while inflation was responsible for higher and higher Hong Kong prices. Today, bargains—for any type of merchandise—are relatively few and far between. Competition among merchants is intense to the point that every consumer—foreign visitors most especially—must take care when shopkeepers offer prices that seem too good to be true; often, that can be the case.

In virtually every retail outlet there's a key word: Bargain, Bargain, Bargain. If it's clothing, try it on and look it over carefully. If it's jewelry, have an expert with you who knows good stuff from shlock, real and cultured pearls from fakes. If it's an appliance, consider how well you might do buying the same article at home, and before purchasing, inspect warranties (are they international?), note serial numbers, play it safe. Ditto watches. (Are you getting the same strap as the sample shown you? Do you trust the merchant with respect to the interior movement of a watch, which, after all, you don't see?) Does the suit or dress you had made fit really well, and is it really well made of the material(s) (including decent thread) that you selected? Are the Italian shoes or neckties actually Italian-made? The point about Hong Kong is that the visitor sticks out like a sore thumb. The canny merchant or salesclerk can invariably size up—but instantly—the kind of customer, or at least prospective customer, he or she is dealing with. Shops have a single goal: profit. The more they sell visitors who leave their shores in a day or a week or two, and live half a world away, the higher their profits. I'm not advising you to beware. But I am saying: Be wary! And no matter the chicness of the shop.

That said, let me point out that there *are* bargains, and of course there *are* many reputable business establishments. (Displaying membership logos of the Hong Kong Tourist Association indicates that they're dues-paying affiliates and presumably ethical.) It's true, too, that imports from the Chinese mainland can be more expensive—easily by a third or a half—than in China (a point worth noting if you'll also be visiting China). But it's also true that much of what the Chinese make is for export only and that if you see something in Hong Kong that you *really* like, play it safe and buy it there, because you may well not come across it in your Chinese travels.

In all events, in the case of an appreciably expensive article, shop around, comparing stocks and prices, before making a decision. Prices do vary. Whenever there's no price tag, bargaining is the rule.

Specifics? The shopping center has caught on, both on Hong Kong and in Kowloon, beyond to the New Territories. Choices are considerably wider than in the past. If you are a compulsive shopper and you want also to see nonmercantile Hong Kong, perhaps making excursions to China and/or Macau, do be sure to allow yourself enough time in Hong Kong. Any visitor at all curious about shops wants a couple of days for them, and easily several days more for additional exploration. By and large, shop personnel are courteous and, of course, English-speaking, and most places accept credit cards.

On Hong Kong Island, the center of the center of the downtown area is the heart of the shopping district—in and around streets like Chater, Des Voeux, and Connaught Road; the Wanchai and Causeway Bay areas, east of Central, also are commercially eminent, with Stanley at the southern tip of the island, important for bargain-laden Stanley Market.

In Kowloon, across Victoria Harbour from Hong Kong Island and reached either by ferry or underground tunnel for cars, taxis, and buses, the bulk of shopping is concentrated in and around the main business street, Nathan Road, and streets running perpendicular to it, like Mody Road, which leads to adjacent and smaller-in-area Tsimshatsui East, with still additional shopping centers. Most visitors have time only to skim the surface with respect to shops. Try, though, to take in a market area, a shopping center (many with fine specialty shops), and a department store. Many shops make it a point to have an outlet on both Hong Kong Island and in Kowloon. With all purchases, insist on receipts, and in the case of appliances and the like, a warranty—preferably one with which you can have the product repaired on home ground if necessary.

SHOPPING CENTERS

Harbour City (edging the Kowloon side of Victoria Harbour) is my favorite because there's virtually nothing you can't buy within its confines—admittedly enormous, and subdivided into three centers—*Ocean Centre, Ocean Galleries,* and *Ocean Terminal.* Don't worry about getting lost; every shop employee, at least in my experience, is not only English-speaking but with a geographical understanding of Harbour City's layout.

New World Center (Salisbury Road, Kowloon—just behind the Regent Hotel) is major league and well located, with such tenants as *Alfred Dunhill, Aquascutum, Cartier, Céline, Charles Jourdan, Givenchy,* and *Louis Férraud*—not to mention a shoe-repair shop!

Pacific Place (Queensway, Central, Hong Kong) is among the newer malls and very smart indeed, with the towering Conrad and Marriott hotels among its immediate neighbors.

Landmark (Des Voeux Road, Central, Hong Kong) is very big: half a dozen floors, mostly with posh boutiques, especially popular with affluent Japanese visitors. Have a look, if only at the windows, of such swank shops as *Giorgio Armani, Jaeger, Kenzo, Loewe, Givenchy, Issey Miyaka, Yves St.-Laurent, Gucci, Lanvin, Meissen, Van Cleef & Arpels, Waterford-Wedgwood,* and *Tiffany*—to give you an idea of this center's caliber.

Shopping centers in the hotels: Hardly to be underestimated, the centers in several major hotels are extensive. That at the *Peninsula Hotel* (Salisbury Road) has 110 shops, on the main floor, mezzanine, and basement; the *Hong Kong Hilton's* center has 75 shops, and those of the *Regent* and *Mandarin Oriental* are substantial, too.

Office buildings with concentrations of shops include *Swire House* (Pedder Street at Connaught Road, Central, Hong Kong), *Prince's Building* (Central, Hong Kong), *Peddar Building* (Central, Hong Kong), as well as *Star House* and the *Silvercord Building*, both on Canton Road, Kowloon. See also the Markets section of this chapter.

ANTIQUES AUCTIONS

Leading international auction houses have Hong Kong branches, with regular sales, the contents of which are available for inspection the day preceding each sale. Hollywood Road is a veritable Antiques Row; I include a number of its shops here, and there are others.

Christie's Swire (Alexandra House, 16 Chater Road, Central, Hong Kong) auctions Chinese ceramics, jade, jewelry, paintings, and other objects.

Sotheby's Hong Kong (502 Exchange Square Two, 8 Connaught Place, Central, Hong Kong) auctions contemporary work as well as antiques.

ANTIQUES SHIPPERS

Michelle International Transport Co., Ltd. (Chung Ying Building, 20 Connaught Road West, Hong Kong) specializes in packing and shipping paintings and antiques and will insure shipments against breakage and other risks.

ANTIQUES AND PAINTINGS

Alvin Lo & Co., Ltd. (314 Exchange Square Two, Central, Hong Kong) makes a specialty of Oriental art.

Ancient Chinese Antiques (199 Hollywood Road, Hong Kong) deals in Chinese pottery, some of it six or seven centuries old.

Art House of Collectors (Des Voeux Commercial Centre, 212 Des Voeux Road, Central, Hong Kong) is worth inspecting for contemporary paintings and drawings by Chinese artists.

Art Treasures Gallery (42 Hollywood Road, Hong Kong) lures with antique Chinese furniture, early Chinese pottery, and other works of art.

Art of China (Omni Hong Kong Hotel Arcade, Canton Road, Kowloon) has lovely jade of considerable age.

C. L. Ma (Yu Yuet Lai Building, 43 Wyndham Street, Hong Kong) deals in both Chinese antique and contemporary hand-crafted furniture.

Harold Wong (Central Building, 1 Pedder Street, Hong Kong) vends beautiful antique Chinese scrolls; paintings, too.

Cheung Hing Tong (227-B Queen's Road, Central, Hong Kong) has curios and paintings as specialties; some from very early dynasties.

Kosilk Hong Kong Co., Ltd. (New World Centre, Kowloon) deals mainly in Korean art and antiques, with some Japanese work, too.

King Feng Arts Co. (Omni Hong Kong Hotel, 3 Canton Road, Kowloon) concentrates on Chinese porcelain snuff bottles; other antiques, too.

Luen Chai Curios (142 Hollywood Road, Hong Kong) deals in Chinese antique porcelain and other works of art.

Martin Fung (Mall, Pacific Place, Phase 2, 88 Queensway, Hong Kong) stocks porcelain figures dating back a thousand years; less aged objects as well.

P. C. Lu and Sons, Ltd. (Omni Hong Kong Hotel, Canton Road, Hong Kong) presents Ming Dynasty antiques—porcelain and otherwise.

Plum Blossoms International Ltd. (305 Exchange Square One, Hong Kong) offers early Ming works—among much else.

Stephen K. Lo (26 Hollywood Road, Hong Kong) is known for exquisite antique panels and other works of art.

Hanlin Gallery (365 Mall, Pacific Place, 88 Queensway, Hong Kong) might be just the place for you to purchase Japanese prints and paintings.

Tai Sing Co. (12 and 22 Wyndham Street, Central, Hong Kong) lures with nineteenth-century porcelains, paintings, bronzes, and furniture; earlier work, as well.

C. Y. Tse Antiques and Collectibles (Hong Kong Hilton Hotel, Central, Hong Kong) is one of the better dealers.

Teresa Colman Fine Arts (37 Wyndham Street, Central, Hong Kong) maintains an unusually diverse stock of embroidered costumes and tapestries, mostly Ching Dynasty, but with work from other dynasties as well: carved-wood sculpture to Tang textiles.

Wan Fung Art Gallery (Star House, 3 Salisbury Road, Kowloon) is exceptionally good for contemporary Chinese paintings, scrolls, and posters.

Y. F. Yang & Co. (Omni Hong Kong Hotel, Canton Road, Kowloon) sells antique glass and porcelain, particularly Chinese snuff bottles.

Yue Po Chai (152 Hollywood Road, Hong Kong) has made its reputation with Asian antiques—gilded Buddha sculptures and cloisonné especially.

Zitah (43 Wyndham Street, Central, Hong Kong) makes a specialty of Qing Dynasty furniture—cupboards, chairs, tables; eighteenth-century scrolls, too.

APPLIANCES

By appliances I mean audio, video, cameras, computers, and accessories for them. Go prepared, ideally, with model numbers that you've brought from home and sufficient background to know your way around in these specialized technical areas. Do enough research to know what prices are like in the U.S.; they may be no higher than in Hong Kong. Be sure model and serial numbers are indicated on your receipt. Insist that you receive the brand-new appliance you've paid for, in original packing, and if it's so bulky or heavy you can't travel with it, ascertain shipping charges in advance of making a purchase; they may cancel out savings. This is a kind of shopping that requires one-upmanship; you must bargain firmly. These shops are mentioned as a convenience for you, rather than as recommendations.

A & A Audio & Video Centre (Hong Kong Hilton Hotel, 2 Queen's Road, Central, Hong Kong).

Union Laservision & Video Centre (Prince's Building, 10 Chater Road and Hang Seng Bank Building, 77 Des Voeux Road—both Central, Hong Kong).

Champagne Radio & Photo Supply (46 Carnarvon Road, Kowloon).

BARBERS/HAIRDRESSERS

Command Performance (12 Pedder Street, Central, Hong Kong; phone 526-5471) is unisex and both its men's barbers and women's hairdressers set fees according to their status: stylist, top stylist; or—the priciest—senior stylist. Manicures, pedicures, coloring—the works. *First Class.*

Mandarin Oriental Hotel Beauty Salon (5 Connaught Road, Central, Hong Kong; phone 522-0111) is big—there are fourteen on staff—and keeps generous hours. Manicures and pedicures, waxing and tinting. Unisex. *Luxury.*

Ambassador Beauty Salon (Ambassador Hotel, 26 Nathan Road, Kowloon; phone 366-9093) is central and cuts men's as well as women's hair. *First Class.*

BOOKS

South China Morning Post Family Bookshops (Ocean Galleries, Harbour City, Kowloon; Ocean Centre, Harbour City, Kowloon; New World Centre, Kowloon; Star Ferry Concourse, Central, Hong Kong; Furama Kempinski Hotel, Connaught Road, Central, Hong Kong; City Plaza II, Tai Koo Shing, Quarry Bay, Hong Kong) maintain large and up-to-the-minute stocks of English-language books.

Commercial Press (9 Yee Wo Street, Causeway Bay, Hong Kong; 28 Wellington Street, Central, Hong Kong; 608 Nathan Road, Mongkok, Kowloon; and Yahohan Stores, New Town Plaza, Shatin, New Territories) is big on paperbacks as well as clothbounds.

Times Book Shop (Hutchison House, Connaught Road, Central, Hong Kong) is conveniently central.

Bookazine, Ltd. is a fair-sized chain with good stocks and outlets at Prince's Building, Central, Hong Kong; Hopewell Centre, Wanchai, Hong Kong; Shui-On Centre, Harbour Road, Wanchai; Shun Tak Centre, Central, Hong Kong;

Alexandra House, Central, Hong Kong; and Jardine House, Connaught Road, Central, Hong Kong.

CAUSEWAY BAY

The name of an area, of course—not a species of shop— Causeway Bay is a Hong Kong Island community east of Central, with the area called Wanchai between these two. I mention Causeway Bay at this point because it's the source not only of a branch of *Lane Crawford* department store and of *China Products*, but also of several clothing-factory outlets and Japanese department stores, (below), not to mention a maze of smaller shops, some in malls, some not. Half a day or an evening (most places are open late) here can be worthwhile.

CHINESE ARTS AND CRAFTS

Before I suggest specific Hong Kong sources for Chinese arts, crafts, cashmere sweaters, and the like, let me note— of interest if you are going to China (Chapter 9)—that prices for Chinese merchandise are considerably cheaper there—in the country of origin—than in Hong Kong, which is, of course, a British territory and (at least until 1997) a foreign country. Withal, the age-old shopper's rule applies in this case as in most: if you see something you can't do without, buy it; you may not come across it in China, which exports jewelry, ceramics, porcelain, and other objects to Hong Kong and other foreign points that are not for sale on home ground—elaborate and expensive objects, in particular. That understood, let me indicate these sources of Chinese goods in Hong Kong:

Chinese Arts & Crafts (30 Canton Road, Kowloon; Shell House, Queen's Road, Central, Hong Kong; 26 Harbour Road, Wanchai, Hong Kong; other locations) is a source of jewelry and quantities of jade, silk, linens, silver objects, cashmere sweaters of a quality that can compare with those of Scotland—not the case with Chinese cashmere eight or nine years ago. To understate: one of Hong Kong's most interesting stores.

Yue Hwa (151 Nathan Road, Kowloon and 301 Nathan Road, Kowloon): The drill here is small stuff fashioned of jade, other jewelry but also clothing and a host of Chinese objects that you'll have fun inspecting, regardless of what you do—or do not—purchase.

Chung Ah (287 Queen's Road, Central, Hong Kong) specializes in fine Chinese porcelain and pottery.

Treasures of China (Furama Kempinski Hotel, Connaught Road, Central, Hong Kong; Mall, Pacific Place, Phase 1, 88 Queensway, Central, Hong Kong) may be exaggerating in its title—but not all that much. Some very nice imports.

Charlotte Horstmann & Gerald Godfrey, Ltd. (Ocean Terminal, Harbour City, Canton Road, Kowloon) was just plain Charlotte Horstmann when I first knew it on earlier Hong Kong visits. You visit this distinguished shop if you're seeking out really ranking Far Eastern pieces—and old ones, at that, the range Tang horses and Korean ceramics through antiques from throughout Asia—India, Burma, and Japan as well as China. An exceptional store.

Jade House (1 Mody Road, Kowloon, with another shop called *C. K. Liang* for the name of the owning family, in the Kowloon Hotel, Middle Road, Kowloon) is long on scene (I remember it from early Hong Kong visits) and with antique and modern jade and allied stoneware its specialties. Some of the work is museum caliber.

Chinese Merchandise Emporium (90 Queen's Road, Central, Hong Kong) is a lovely old-fashioned name for a shop fairly brimming with Chinese merchandise, some of it exceptional.

Hong Kong Welfare Handicrafts (Salisbury Road, Kowloon) vends a variety of craft objects created by clients of welfare agencies in the territory. You may well find something you like.

CLOTHING—CUSTOM-MADE

On my first trip to Hong Kong, years back, custom-made suits alone made a visit obligatory. They were a real steal— cheaper than what we paid for factory-made clothing at home. And they were often ready in two or three or four days at most. All that has changed. Prices have in recent years risen appreciably with steep inflation, while at the same time the value of the American dollar has dropped. My advice is that you have clothing custom-made in Hong Kong *only* if you've a figure not easily fit with ready-made garments.

Count on several fittings (most tailors like three but will let you get away with two if they would otherwise lose the sale); expect no one at home to recognize that you're wearing a custom-made garment (they look no classier than our decent-quality ready-made) and take adequate time selecting materials; tailors generally have a number of fabric swatch books.

Bargaining is the hard and firm rule; insist on a lower price per garment if you're ordering more than one. And shop around before selecting a tailor. There are no two alike and if I can make any generalization it's that tailors *not* located in hotels (especially better hotels) tend to be less expensive for the simple reason that rents are usually lower and they're not as easy to seek out as the tailor down a few floors in your hostelry.

It's always wise—and cheaper—if you take possession of what you've ordered while in Hong Kong, rather than have it shipped. First, because you'll be present for the final fitting, and second, because chances are you'll pay no duty upon arrival in the U.S. with the garment, while you well may, if it's shipped. Let me repeat, ladies' garments, men's suits, sport jackets or slacks, whatever: be sure that you'll be in Hong Kong long enough, ideally for three fittings, minimally for two. If not, *don't* order custom-made clothing, which in any event—please note—I want to repeat that I recommend only to persons with hard-to-fit figures requiring considerable alterations in the case of off-the-peg garments.

Hong Kong tailors, incidentally, divide themselves into three clothing categories: Shanghai (considered the best), Canton (No. 2) and Indian (No. 3). (If they're Chinese, they'll invariably tell you they're from Shanghai.)

Here's a clutch of custom tailors, mostly catering to women as well as to men. Before you select one, insist on seeing some of his work. And I repeat: shop around and bargain firmly.

A-Man Hing Cheong (Mandarin Oriental Hotel, Connaught Road, Central, Hong Kong), "Amen" to his fans, is ideal for the visitor who is not only affluent (suits and shirts are more expensive than at many of the other tailors) but who will be in town a week.

Hong Shing (Shop LI-14, New World Centre, Salisbury Road, Kowloon) is conveniently located, advanced in age (it opened in 1932, its card avers) and with good prices.

House Tailor (Level 2, New World Centre, Salisbury Road, Kowloon) has prices that are among the lowest of any tailor researched for these pages.

Jimmy Chen (Peninsula Hotel, Salisbury Road, Kowloon; Edinburgh Tower, Queen's Road, Central, Hong Kong; other locations) is among the more expensive of the tailors. But—and I speak from experience—be sure to check your purchases carefully to see that they're made just as you ordered them. This is a shop that I patronized on one occasion—but will not, again.

Johnson Dong (Hong Kong Hotel, Kowloon) is anxious enough to please that he puts the phone number of his workshop/home on his business card, as well as the showroom address and phone.

Kawa (Prince's Building, Chater Road, Hong Kong): I learned about this fine tailor from Thomas Axmacher, general manager of the Regent Hotel and easily one of the best-dressed GMs in town. Expensive.

Mode Elegante (Peninsula Hotel, Salisbury Road, Kowloon) is not the only tailor in the Peninsula, but my researches indicate its prices are among the most reasonable.

Paramount Tailor Co. (Shop 43, Level One, New World Shopping Mall, Salisbury Road, Kowloon) makes its garments on the spot—you see the table where material is cut—at good prices and with a pleasant staff.

Princeton (71 Peking Road, Kowloon)—if eager-beaver appearing (salesmen seem ready to pounce as a prospective customer enters)—is big enough to promise delivery in two to three days.

Robert Tailor (Mandarin Oriental Hotel, Connaught Road, Central, Hong Kong) is fairly pricey but has lots of repeat fans.

Stephen Lo (Shop L2-40, New World Centre, Salisbury Road, Kowloon) prices his suits and shirts reasonably; those I have seen are super.

Tak Tak (Shop 38C, L2, New World Centre, Salisbury Road, Kowloon) is surely the most memorably named tailor in town. And its tabs are appealing.

Ying Tai (Hong Kong Hilton Hotel, Queen's Road, Central, Hong Kong): I came across Ying Tai's big shop in the course of a stay at the Hilton and liked the staff and the clothes. Good quality.

CUSTOM-MADE SHIRTS

A-Man Hing Cheong (Mandarin Oriental Hotel, 5 Connaught Road, Central, Hong Kong) is where my friend Stephen Wong of the Hong Kong Tourist Association has his shirts made. Very nice. Suits, too (above).

Ascot Chang (Prince's Building, Chater Road, Central, Hong Kong, with branches in the Regent and Peninsula hotels in Kowloon), like Kawa Tailors (above) came to my attention through Thomas Axmacher of the Regent Hotel. Chang shirts are surely the spiffiest (and among the priciest) in town. Two fittings.

David's (Mandarin Oriental Hotel), Connaught Road, Central, Hong Kong, and also at 33 Kimberley Road, Kowloon) begins with good-looking shirtings and continues with really smart finished products, selected from one of their own styles or copied from a shirt you bring in. You want two fittings.

Shanghai Waiwing (Shop L2-25B, New World Centre, Salisbury Road, Kowloon) will make men's shirts in a single day (if you place the order before midmorning) and the price goes down if you order at least half a dozen. Suits, of course, take longer. A nice shop.

Takly (Hong Kong Hilton Hotel, Central, Hong Kong) is among the better shirtmakers, fabrics through fit.

CLOTHING—READY-MADE

Alfred Dunhill (Mall, Pacific Place, 88 Queensway, Hong Kong) is a branch of the New York-based—and distinguished—men's clothiers and haberdashers.

Bello (404 Pedder Building, 12 Pedder Street, Central, Hong Kong): I would think, because this shop is for women's clothing only, its name would be the feminine *Bella* rather than the masculine *Bello*. Ah, well, a rose by...

Benetton (Mall, Pacific Place, 88 Queensway, Hong Kong): You are never—even in the Far Pacific—far from Benetton.

Cerruti 1881 (Peninsula Hotel, Kowloon) is the well-known Paris-origin men's toggery, with a good selection for its friends in Asia. Very pricey.

Chanel (Peninsula Hotel, Kowloon) is a source not only of its famed perfumes and colognes but of clothing accessories, too—and at a price. How about U.S. $100 for a necktie?

China Town (25 and 39 Stanley Main Street, Stanley, Hong Kong) is a super stop for men's sport shirts and sweaters, cashmere especially.

Diane Freis (Unit A1, 10th Floor, Kaiser Estate, Phase 1, 412 Man Yue Street, Hunghom, Kowloon): That long address is worth noting; it's the location of the factory outlet of a Hong Kong-based American who has become one of the territory's hottest women's designers. (There are half a dozen standard-price Freis outlets—one at the Mall, Pacific Place, 88 Queensway, Hong Kong; another at Ocean Galleries, Harbour City, Kowloon—but why pay more?)

Four Seasons (51 Man Yue Street, in the Kaiser Estate area of Hunghom, Kowloon) just might have a bargain or two in silk that will interest you; men's and women's shirts; lots of additional women's wear. Stock is mostly overruns and samples from local factories.

Façonnable (200A Ocean Terminal, Kowloon) is a branch of a France-based chain (see *France at Its Best)* that designs some of the planet's most beautiful neckties—and other men's wear as well. Expensive.

Fulam Lam Kee Trading Co. (49 Stanley Main Street, Stanley, Hong Kong) is at once a good source of leather handbags and luggage, and of sportswear, Levi shirts included.

Daniel Hechter (Prince's Building, Central, Hong Kong) is a source not only of the haute-design Hechter clothing out of France, but of that of the late Italian designer, Valentino, as well.

Gieves & Hawkes (Prince's Building, Central, Hong Kong) is one of those rare British clothiers with a Hong Kong branch, selling "By Appointment" not only to Queen Elizabeth II but also to her husband, Prince Philip, and her son, Prince Charles. Conservatively spiffy—and costly.

Joseph Ho (Mall, Pacific Place, 88 Queensway, Hong Kong) takes its name from one of Hong Kong's top women's designers. Have a look.

Hugo Boss (Mall, Pacific Place, 88 Queensway, Hong Kong), I learned in the course of researching *Germany at Its Best*, is not one but a trio of Germans, who own this international chain vending stylish men's duds.

ItalModa (30 Man Yue Street, Kaiser Estates, Hunghom, Kowloon) is a source of cut-rate silks—shirts for men, shirts and other clothing for the ladies. Nice.

Jermyn Street Limited is not on Jermyn Street—that's in London—but rather in the Peninsula Hotel, Kowloon, and at Swire House and Prince's Building in Hong Kong. It sells Daks trousers and other quality menswear.

Kenzo (Peninsula Hotel, Kowloon) is an esteemed albeit pricey Japan-based firm with its own-design women's clothes the draw.

Ricci (Peninsula Hotel basement, Kowloon): If my calculations were correct at the time of writing, Ricci's ties went for a hundred U.S. bucks per cravat.

Shirt Stop (Pedder Building, 12 Pedder Street, Hong Kong, and other locations) very cleverly has a logo that puts you immediately in mind of the London Underground logo. So of course you stop in. Men's shirts are real buys here.

Signature (Kaiser Estate, Man Yue Street, Hunghom, Kowloon) is not, to be sure, very friendly, but it does have excellent buys in clothing—men's suits and other garments with the Joseph Ho label (see above); Ho women's blouses, suits, and shoes, too. Worth a visit.

Timothy (Kaiser Estate, Man Yue Street, Hunghom, Kowloon, and other locations) specializes in direct-from-the-factory silk blouses and suits. Its men's wear is quality stuff, too—bargain-tabbed and including wool sport jackets, zipper jackets, and Italian leather belts.

Vica Moda (Kaiser Estate, Man Yue Street, Hunghom, Kowloon, and other locations) specializes in direct-from-the factory silk, cashmere, cotton, and linen clothing, men's and women's both, generally at modest prices.

Wong Lin Wah (Stanley Main Street, Stanley, Hong Kong) has good-value clothing, men's shirts especially.

Yves St. Laurent (Mall, Pacific Place, 88 Queensway, Central, Hong Kong) is a Hong Kong outlet for the Paris-based designer's women's ready-to-wear.

Wintex Fashions (Room 401, 12 Pedder Street, Central, Hong Kong) can be worth the elevator ride, especially for all-wool sweaters—lambswool as well as cashmere—at good prices. Other men's and women's clothing, too.

DEPARTMENT STORES

Lane Crawford (Queen's Road, Central, Hong Kong; 74 Nathan Road, Kowloon; Pacific Place, 88 Queensway, Central, Hong Kong) leads the list because it leads the department stores—on scene as long as I remember visiting Hong Kong: full-service, British-style (the British know how to run department stores, see *Britain at Its Best*), courteously staffed, and efficient.

Marks & Spencer (Cityplaza, King's Road, Quarry Bay, Hong Kong; Harbour City, Canton Road, Kowloon; and Mong Kok, Kowloon) is about as well known to American travelers to Britain (it has branches in most cities) as Buckingham Palace, and with its three stores here as popular in Hong Kong as on home base. Go for clothing (the same house-brand items you know from Britain) groceries, cosmetics.

Dodwell (Landmark, Central, Hong Kong, and with a number of branches) is big on moderately priced duds for the family, but there are other things to spend your money on, too.

Mitsukoshi (500 Hennessy Road, Causeway Bay, Hong Kong) is one of the Japanese department stores clustered in Causeway Bay—none of them inexpensive, but the lot with interesting merchandise, as for example, at Mitsukoshi, where the range is costume jewelry through groceries, with heavy emphasis on home furnishings and clothes at varying price levels, budget to big bucks.

Daimaru (Paterson Street, Causeway Bay, Hong Kong) comprises a pair of buildings and is of Japanese origin. You will probably want to concentrate on what I call the clothing building—its wares are Japanese and temptingly priced, but Japanese housewares may be of interest, too.

EYEGLASSES

Eyeglasses in Hong Kong can cost two-thirds less than in the United States. Ideally, you have a copy of your prescription with you; if not, make sure that it's an accredited optician or optometrist who determines your prescription from the glasses you're wearing. Allow a couple of days, of course trying out new glasses in the shop to make sure there are no distortions in your vision. Optical shops in Hong Kong are about as common as fast-food joints in New York, and not everybody wearing a long white coat in these shops is an optician; ask the person waiting on you for his or her qualifications, and insist on an optician for fitting and of course an optometrist for testing. Contact-lens wearers tell me that savings on contacts are nothing like so substantial as for glasses.

Optical Shop is the name of a chain that simply has to be among the world's largest, in terms at least of retail outlets. The shop in Prince's Building (10 Chater Street, Central, Hong Kong) is staffed with both opticians and optometrists, and service in my experience has been cheerful, professional, and prompt. (Other Optical Shop locations include Man Yee Building, 67 Queen's Road, Central, Hong Kong; 258 Shun Tak Centre, Connaught Road, Central, Hong Kong; Mall, Pacific Place, 88 Queensway, Central, Hong Kong; Ocean Terminal, Harbour City, Canton Road, Kowloon; Star House, Salisbury Road, Kowloon; Kowloon Hotel, Nathan Road, Kowloon.

Hong Kong Optical is another chain, although it's considerably smaller than Optical Shop. Its outlets include those at Central Building, 21 Queen's Road, Central, Hong Kong; 10 D'Aguilar Street, Central, Hong Kong; Ambassador Hotel, Nathan Road, Kowloon; and Houston Centre, 63 Mody Road, Kowloon.

Optical 88 is still another chain, with locations including Century Square, 1 D'Aguilar Street, Central, Hong Kong; Ocean Terminal, Harbour City, Canton Road, Kowloon; and 181 Nathan Road, Kowloon.

JEWELRY

Hong Kong is a jewelry manufacturing—and diamond cutting—center of global importance; it's literally dotted with jewelry shops. Prices are good, thanks to exemption from local duty and tax. It's worth my noting at this point that you may take *un*set gems into the United States at virtually no duty (or no duty at all), but that you *will* pay duty for *finished* jewelry—rings, bracelets, brooches, necklaces, jeweled watches, and the like. Important, too, is the fact that Hong Kong gold pieces are often 18-carat rather than the 14-carat (and less yellow) generally favored by Americans. You want to specify which you prefer when dealing with jewelers; 14-carat is cheaper than 18-carat. And note that diamonds, pearls, and opals can be very good buys.

Receipts are important for U.S. Customs; you are, as you know, limited to $400 duty-free in purchases. If you've purchased gold objects, have the number of carats specified. And if you know the type of jewelry you'll want to buy, price comparable pieces in the U.S. before leaving home for a good idea of the markets, Hong Kong vs. U.S.

Jewelers are a category of merchants who can be reliable in hotels; with many complaints, managers would not renew their leases. Here are a few:

Bulgari (Peninsula Hotel, Salisbury Road, Kowloon; and Landmark Building, Hong Kong) is the very same you may know from its stores in New York, Europe, and Japan. Distinctively designed—and costly—jewelry and watches.

Cartier, the Paris-origin jeweler with shops worldwide, has no fewer than five outlets in Hong Kong: Prince's Building, Pacific Place, Peninsula Hotel, Regent Hotel, and Empire Centre. Pricey watches as well as fine jewelry.

Gemsland (Hong Kong Hilton and Mandarin Oriental hotels, both Central, Hong Kong) deals in a range of gems, gold and pearls as well—in quantity.

Kai Yin Lo (Mandarin Oriental Hotel, Connaught Road, Central, Hong Kong)—original gold-based designs, by the designer-owner.

Kevin (Holiday Inn Golden Mile, 50 Nathan Road, Kowloon): big stocks, considerable variety.

Ritz Jewelry and Watch Co. (Hong Kong Hilton Hotel, Central, Hong Kong)—timepieces as well as fine jewels.

Tiffany, New York's best-known jeweler, has two Hong Kong stores: one in the Landmark Building in Hong Kong and the other in the Peninsula Hotel, Kowloon. Diamonds and other precious stones, expensive watches.

Van Cleef & Arpels, which you'll no doubt remember from locations in New York, Paris, Geneva, Palm Beach, and Beverly Hills, has a quartet of Hong Kong shops: in the Peninsula and Regent hotels, Kowloon; 2 Pacific Place and the Landmark, both in Hong Kong.

LUXURY IMPORTS

The kind of baubles you would buy on Madison Avenue in New York, Chicago's North Michigan, the D.C. suburbs, Rodeo Drive in Beverly Hills, London's Bond Street, Paris's Faubourg Ste.-Honoré, Rome's Via Condotti—by that I mean European haute couture, bags, neckties, shoes, jewelry from globally famed designers—are all available in Hong Kong, with a single firm often maintaining two or three branches in different parts of town. The shops are beautiful, ditto the merchandise. But I want to caution you not only that it's expensive, but for as long as the American dollar remains weak, *more* expensive, by and large, than in the United States, (except, of course, that there's no sales tax, which can be substantial on big purchases in the U.S.). These big-bucks items are mainly for the wealthy Japanese market (many Japanese go to Hong Kong on shopping weekends; and in more than one boutique it's easier to communicate with sales staff in Japanese than in English; indeed, you can come across shops with Japanese but not English spoken).

The shops of the Peninsula Hotel—which constitute a major shopping center with respect to quantity (110) as well as quality—give you a good idea of what I mean by blue-chip boutiques in Hong Kong. They include, to name some, *Le Must de Cartier, Christian Dior, Hermès, Bulgari, Ascot Chang Shirtmakers, Mode Élégante Tailors, Waterford-Wedgwood, Tiffany, Gieves & Hawkes, Cerruti 1881, Céline, Nina Ricci, Alfred Dunhill, Joyce* (a leading Hong Kong women's shop), *Gucci, Polo Ralph Lauren, Loewe, Bally, Chanel, Van Cleef & Arpels, Gianni Versace,* and the Peninsula's own shop with Peninsula-logo gifts. The Regent and Hong Kong Hilton hotels' shops are similarly classy.

MARKETS

Hong Kong markets are fun and frequently yield bargains. You can spend an entire vacation exploring them, but I would concentrate on these:

Stanley Market (Stanley Main Street, Stanley, Hong Kong)—on the south-central tip of Hong Kong Island—is the best known and with good reason. It's easy to negotiate—the geography cooperates—and you do indeed find bargains—a Hong Kong-made Gap chambray shirt for a third of its U.S. price (the label has been slashed almost in half; canvas luggage and flight bags to carry home what you've purchased while in Hong Kong; amusing things for kids; linen and leather, tees and sweats, shirts and sweaters that are locally made discontinued models with labels readable albeit slashed.

Jade Market (Battery and Kansa streets, Kowloon)—so long as you don't expect to snag really precious stuff—is another requisite. There is some good jade and all dealers are presumably certified by their merchants' association. Look at all the carts as you amble along. It goes without saying that you bargain—and no nonsense about it. If you've a Chinese friend or colleague who knows jade—if it's good quality it should be translucent with no mistaking clarity of color—and will accompany you, you're in luck. But have a look, even on your own.

Temple Street Market (Temple Street, Kowloon) is unique in that it's evenings only, from 8 P.M. until about midnight. You go at least as much for atmosphere as merchandise (don't make a visit on an evening when you're going off to a posh restaurant and are in dressy duds). Merchants vend primarily for your ordinary everyday Hong Kong family— budgety clothing for mom, dad, and the kids, inexpensive bags and baggage, assorted doodads, some of which make amusing gifts. The scene as you move along is Hong Kong at its least glamorous—tooth-pullers and acupuncturists, musicians and mah-jongg players. Memorable.

Kowloon Market (see under Produce, below).

PHARMACIES

Watson's is an extensive Hong Kong–wide chain with considerable outlets including 100 Nathan Road, Kowloon; and in the Hong Kong Hilton Hotel, Queen's Road, Central Hong Kong. Lots of nonpharmaceutical items, too.

Manning Dispensary Ltd. is a chain, too, bigger on Hong Kong Island than Kowloon, where its shop is at Ocean Galleries, Harbour City, Canton Road. Hong Kong locations include the Landmark Building and Swire House on Chater Road, both Central.

PORCELAIN, POTTERY, CRYSTAL

Hunter's (Peninsula and Kowloon hotels and Ocean Terminal at Harbour City, all in Kowloon; Mall, Pacific Place, 88 Queensway; and Repulse Bay restaurant-shop complex, Repulse Bay, Hong Kong) is a porcelain shop extraordinaire—Germany's Meissen, England's Wedgwood, Italy's Richard Ginori, France's Sèvres—to name the principal brands. Needless to say, very expensive. And of course they ship.

Meissen (Landmark, Central, Hong Kong) is an outpost of the distinguished German porcelain manufacturer. Go, if you're at all interested in beautiful china.

Pottery Workshop (2 Lower Albert Road, Hong Kong) concentrates on imaginative contemporary work, frequent short-term exhibits by Hong Kong designers. Have a look.

Richard Ginori (Mall, Pacific Place, 88 Queensway, Central, Hong Kong) deals in the best-known of Italy's porcelains.

Royal Doulton (Mall, Pacific Place, 88 Queensway, Central, Hong Kong) is no doubt already familiar to you as one of Britain's great china houses.

Royal Copenhagen and its fellow-Danish firm, *Georg Jensen,* are both on scene. The former, Royal Copenhagen, is at Ocean Terminal, Harbour City, Kowloon, and Prince's

Building, Chater Road, Hong Kong, and claims to sell the famous Danish china at 15 percent less than in the United States, and of course without sales taxes so common in the U.S. *Georg Jensen* (Mall, Pacific Place, Phase 2, 88 Queensway, Hong Kong), is chockablock with the snazzy silver bearing its name. Have a look, if you can, at both shops.

Waterford/Wedgwood (Peninsula Hotel, Salisbury Road, Kowloon; Landmark, Central, Hong Kong; and other locations) sell two splendid lines—Wedgwood china out of England, and Waterford crystal from Ireland.

PRODUCE

Kowloon Market (Marketplace): I don't expect that you'll be purchasing fruits and vegetables in enough quantity to visit this teeming market. You make the trip simply to have a look at the proceedings. This is one of Hong Kong's great shows. And it's completely spontaneous, with sellers at myriad stalls, the stars. Go early in the morning, about 8 A.M., when the market is at its busiest.

SHOES—CUSTOM-MADE

If this is a new experience, note that you start with leather—ideally of your selection—following with the model (bring one of your own shoes to be copied, if you like, or select from those in the shop). You usually pay half the price as a deposit. Make sure you'll be in Hong Kong long enough to try on the finished products, so necessary adjustments can be made on the spot. Considering what factory-made shoes cost at home, prices are not bad.

Lily (Peninsula Hotel, Salisbury Road, Kowloon); *Kow Hoo Shoes Co.* (Hong Kong Hilton Hotel, Central, Hong

Kong); and *VIP Shoes* (Regent Hotel, Salisbury Road, Kowloon) constitute a worth-a-visit trio.

SHOE REPAIR

Mister Minit (Queen's Road, opposite the Hong Kong Hilton, and Ocean Centre—third floor—in the Harbour Centre shopping center complex, Canton Road, Kowloon).

SILK

Old Peking Silk Co. (219 Nathan Road, Kowloon) has fabulous selections of mostly Chinese silks by the meter —worth knowing about for women who will be having clothing custom-made while in Hong Kong, or to take home.

SPORTING GOODS

Marathon Sports Ltd. is a multi-unit chain, well stocked for a considerable variety of athletic diversions. Locations include Upper Ground, Center Square, Hong Kong; and Ocean Terminal, Harbour City, Kowloon.

WATCHES

Well-known makes are sold by authorized dealers at prices usually less than at home—and with no sales tax. But there are brands you never heard of—handsome and selling for as little as $50, which can be terrific; I'm the satisfied owner of one such. Although Hong Kong merchants— given the quantity of competition—are generally kind and gracious, certain of the watch shops on Nathan Road, the main Kowloon street—can be unpleasant. When you find this is the case, exit immediately; there are plenty of other stores nearby.

Carol's Watch and Jewelry (Ocean Terminal, Harbour City, Canton Road, Kowloon) is a good source of brand-name timepieces.

Dickson Watch and Jewelry (Peninsula Hotel, Salisbury Road, Kowloon) specializes in pricey makes—Givenchy, Guy La Roche, S.T. Dupont, and Rolex among them.

May's Jewelry & Watch Co. (46 Nathan Road, Kowloon) is one of the nice watch shops on Nathan Road, where, as I have indicated, watch dealers can be disagreeable. Ask for Simon Chan.

Toyotsu (86 Nathan Road, Kowloon) sells name-brand watches in tremendous variety, as well as pearls and gold necklaces. Customers are mainly Japanese but the staff, in my experience, has been English-speaking and cordial.

Zürich (91 Nathan Road, Kowloon) is an ideal name for a watch shop, if ever there was one. They sell Rolex and Patek Philippe from Switzerland, but watches from other lands—Japan's Seiko, for example—as well.

6

Macau to See

They have both—I refer to Macau as well as Hong Kong—grown since my first acquaintance with each. But I seem to recall that in those earlier encounters each was a relatively low-key colony of a European power—Hong Kong, of course, British; Macau, Portuguese. Well, I don't want to imply that time has stood still in Macau while Hong Kong has boomed. But Macau remains—much to its credit, in my view—smaller and less hectic and more relaxing than its bigger neighbor.

My point is that each is visit-worthy in its own distinctive way. Macau is a delightful diversion for the traveler who's been shopping without surcease in Hong Kong. Not that the shopping is not good value, as well, in Macau. But it makes a point—and with success—of encouraging visitors to unwind, the while offering them a not inconsiderable sampling—Chinese temples and Christian churches, casinos and gardens, museums and fortresses—of a history extending back four and a half centuries.

LAY OF THE LAND

The central area—and yes, it's called Downtown—is anchored by an east-west thoroughfare, Avenida Almeida Ri-

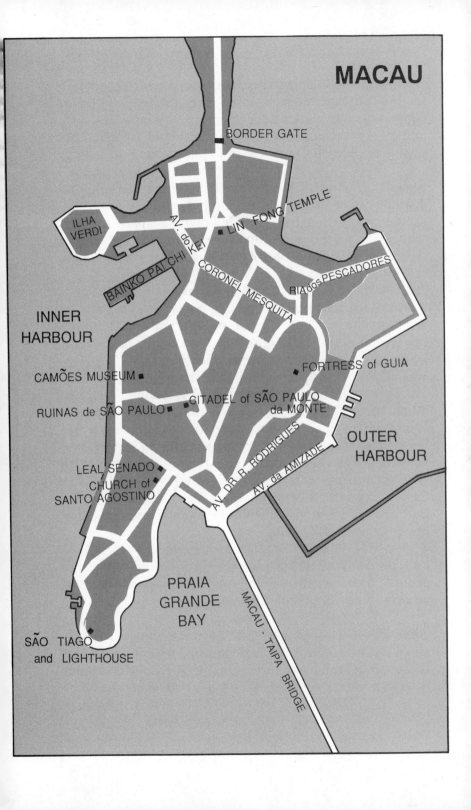

bero, with the main square, Largo do Senado—your visit might coincide with one of the frequent open-air concerts—in its center, and shops, restaurants, churches, and other visitable monuments dotted about, on a number of streets (Rua de Campo is an important one) including:

Ruins of St. Paul's Church (Rua de São Paulo)—a splendid seventeenth-century facade believed to have been designed by an Italian Jesuit and built with a Japanese Christian work force—is Macau's trademark. The fire that destroyed most of the rest of the church took place in 1935.

Leal Senado (Avenida Almeida Ribero) is Macau's originally sixteenth-century showplace public building, and is, in effect, its city council, a not unimportant function for a not unimportant building, entered via a pair of gardens, with the second—whose surprise masterwork is a spherical sculpture on which are indicated the routes of the long-ago Portuguese who were the first Europeans to explore much of the world. The up-a-flight Senate Chamber's walls—with crystal chandeliers, red damask draperies, and bas-reliefs whose theme is Portuguese-Macau history—are its strong point. (There are twenty-two senators plus a seventeen-member Legislative Assembly.) Macau's *Public Library*, in the same building, is justifiably celebrated for its decor—a masterful mix of woodcarving and a chandeliered ceiling in gold and white.

Camoes Museum (Praça Luis de Camoes) makes a specialty of Chinese art—paintings, sculpture, porcelain, and a perfectly lovely art-filled garden.

Taipa House Museum (Avenida da Praia, village of Taipa, easily reached by frequently departing buses from Macau) is the grand mansion museum of Macau, an authentically—and tastefully—restored early-twentieth-century house of a substantial Eurasian family, with fine locally made, Chinese-influenced Western furnishings in parlors, dining room, and bedrooms.

Sé (Largo da Sé) is the shortest word for cathedral in any language with which I am familiar. This is a looker of a nineteenth-century Baroque structure, with an especially felicitous double-tower facade, which is a successor to the first cathedral dating to the seventeenth century. The current building went up in 1850, was almost obliterated by a typhoon a quarter century later, and restored on more than one occasion, most recently in 1937. Go inside if only for the stained glass.

Church of Santo Agostinho (Largo de Santo Agostinho): If you've time to visit but one church after the cathedral, Santo Agostinho should be your choice. It's an early-nineteenth-century successor to a sixteenth-century original. Elaborate white pilasters encircle the high altar, with the painted green ceilings punctuated by crystal chandeliers, and walls of palest yellow. Once you've had a look, it's not difficult to understand why this church is often selected for Macau's most fashionable weddings.

Church of São Lourenço (Rua de São Lourenço), though founded in the sixteenth century, makes its home in an early-nineteenth-century stone building fringed by a palm-dotted garden. You don't want to skip the interior—fine statue of St. Lawrence on the high altar, turquoise ceiling accented with gilded beams, good stained glass.

Church of São Tiago de Barra, (Pousada de São Tiago)—named for the military protector of Macau—is a little chapel that went up as long ago as 1740, and is attached to the pousada, or inn, based on the foundations of a venerable fort. Standouts are the white and blue tile designs, not to mention a statue of the saint—James—for whom the church is named.

Church of São Domingos (Largo de São Domingos) replaces a late sixteenth-century predecessor, and is among Macau's oldest churches. It opened in the early seventeenth century, and attracts passersby with its stone facade accented by green shutters. Go in to observe a veritable network of saints in carved ivory, a pale albeit beautiful statue of the Virgin and Child on the high altar, and a little museum of historic church objects.

Fortress of São Tiago de Barra (Avenida da Republica) is, hands down, Macau's most enjoyable fortress—if indeed a fortress can be so termed—because it's currently the site of one of the territory's leading restaurants. Barra, as it's called by locals, originated in 1629, and was considered so important that its commanders in the early centuries were appointed by the Portuguese kings rather than by local governors. Came World War II and the fort's cannon were sold to feed refugees from Hong Kong—a signal for the beginning of the demolition of much of the complex. What remains today—chapel, cistern turned fountain, original walls—is eminently visitable (and, as I point out in Chapter 8, the food is good).

Coloane and Taipa Islands are what you might call dependencies of Macau and easily reached from it by regularly departing ferries. As I mention in an earlier paragraph, Taipa's absolute requisite is a visit to *Taipa House Museum*, but there are, as well, colonial-style Portuguese houses, intimate-in-scale Buddhist temples, the *University of East Asia* campus, and Asia's first harness-racing track. Coloane's beaches (with pool, restaurant, and changing rooms) are attractive to Macau—and other—visitors. *St.*

Francis Xavier Chapel (Coloane Park) with a walk-through aviary is charming.

Casinos: Of the four *casinos*, that called Lisboa never closes; the others are Macau Palace, Jai-Alai, and Oriental; at all, you may try your luck at baccarat, blackjack, boule, craps, fan-tan, and slot machines, most of which gobble up both Macau and Hong Kong coins. (If you win at the casino—or even if you don't—there's more betting to be done—at both harness and greyhound racing tracks, the latter on Taipa Island, the former on Avenida General Castelo Branco on Macau.)

Citadel of São Paulo da Monte (Rua da Citadel) is high enough up to afford fine views of town and sea, and if you go on a weekend you're welcomed at the entrance by students attired in natty eighteenth-century uniforms. The four-century-old Citadel's principal moment of glory was when it was the site of a Portuguese defeat of Dutch invaders in 1622. Its Jesuit architect-builders erected it in the heart of town, flanked on either side by the city wall.

Fortress of Guia, guarding Macau from its highest point since 1638, has two attributes: a lighthouse that's the oldest on the coast of China, in service since it was completed in 1865, atop Guia Hill, which is the site, as well, of a *chapel* with a bell whose inscription indicates that it dates to 1707. Note its buttressed walls and vaulted ceiling.

Kun Iam Temple (Avenida da Coronel Mesquita) is actually a cluster of temples, but it's usually only the main building that's open—as well it should be, given its porcelain friezes and trio of altars (including one with a gilded Buddha). This is a historic place: it's where, in 1844, the United States signed its first treaty of friendship and trade with China. Take your time as you amble about this seventeenth-century Ming-era masterwork, whose treasures extend from the pair of temple lions guarding it, through a statue of Marco Polo, and the granite table where the U.S.-China treaty was signed. Out back, there's a honey of a garden.

A-Ma Temple (Inner Harbor), parts of which go back to the fourteenth century, is important not only because of its advanced age, but because its early name—*A Ma Gao*—came to be pronounced *Macau* by the Portuguese, who later officially changed the spelling to conform to the pronunciation.

Protestant Cemetery (Praça Luis de Camoes), next door to the Camoes Museum (above) is not easy for English-speakers to miss: a sign above its entrance identifies it as the "East India Company Old Protestant Cemetery, 1814." Its chapel is the site of English-language Anglican services conducted on Sunday mornings the year round. Europeans from a number of countries, as well as Americans, are buried in the cemetery. You get an idea of the history of Macau as you read the legends on its gravestones. Pay your respects.

7

Macau to Stay

HOTELS: MACAU'S DELIGHTFUL SURPRISE

Time does indeed fly. I recall that on my initial visit to Macau a couple of decades back, there wasn't a hotel that I could term top rung. Today, though, its hotels are Macau's secret touristic weapon. Don't deny yourself the pleasure of staying a night or two, with contemporary creature comforts so tempting. Here's a rundown:

Mandarin Oriental Macau Hotel (Avenida da Amizade; phone 956-1110)—a sister-hotel of the Mandarin Oriental Hong Kong, where you may well have stayed, or will stay—is a smart and stark white high rise at the seawall of Macau's Outer Harbor, convenient to the arrival terminal from Hong Kong and to shops and casinos, as well. First surprise—in so contemporary a setting—is a traditional-style Portuguese-decor lobby centered by a splendid carved-teak staircase. But rooms are special, too, teak-furnished with fabrics from Portugal and views either of the romantic Guia Fortress or the South China Sea. I'm a stickler for the Mandarin restaurants, the Grill especially, but the Dynasty's Chinese dishes are hardly to be despised. Café Girassol is casual and tasty, and come the evening you may dance or simply sit and sip in Bar da Guia. Execs appreciate the top-of-the-line business center and the meeting rooms. Guests of all ages go for the pool and health center (with tennis and squash supplementing it). The casino is one of Macau's smartest. Super service throughout—and I speak from experience. Member, Leading Hotels of the World. *Luxury.*

Hyatt Regency Macau Hotel (Estrada Almirante Marques Esparteiro, Taipa Island; phone 321-1234): What it comes down to is that if the Hyatt Regency doesn't have it, you're not likely to find it on Macau. This modern, 11-floor, 353-room-and-suite house welcomes you in a tile-floored, high-ceilinged lobby. Rooms—meticulously equipped, the range alarm clocks to smoke-alarm detectors—have all been recently refurbished in pastel tones. Setting is three gardened acres. There's a well-equipped business center and no fewer than four restaurants (Portuguese and Chinese among them) and as many cafés and bars (including one you may swim up to, edging the pool), top floor of extra-tab, extra-amenity Regency Club rooms, beauty salon/barber shop. On scene, too, are a small casino, tennis and squash, as well as, a unisex hairdresser, a really big pool, a child-care center (with fabulous stuffed dogs that adults are at least as partial to as kids are), and an outdoor playground. Very nice indeed. *Luxury.*

Pousada de São Tiago (Avenida da Republica; phone 378-111) occupies the fabulous seventeenth-century Fortress of São Tiago da Barra, about which I write with enthusiasm on an earlier page. The old fort has been deftly converted into what I consider Macau's best hotel, with but 23 no-two-alike rooms and suites, all looking onto the sea, and most with balconies. Decor is Portuguese-inspired, dominantly mahogany, pink marble, and blue-and-white tiles. Albeit with all the comforts of an up-to-the-minute hostelry—direct-dial phones, individual temperature control and air conditioning, mini-fridge, remote-control telly, and well-appointed baths. Friendly, too. *Luxury.*

Pousada Ritz (Rua da Boa Vista; phone 339-955) compensates for its away-from-the-center situation with good looks and superior facilities. This is a modern house with a hint of the traditional Orient in its decor. It's small—there are but 31 capacious, individually decorated rooms and suites, with super baths; but there's a Chinese restaurant—Lijinxuan by name—that's among the best and most beautiful in town, with drinks available in the bar—or my choice, at an al fresco table in the Terrace Garden Café. And talk about recreation centers: the Ritz's embraces a handsome pool edged by black and white tile columns, billiard and dart rooms, well-equipped gym, sauna and whirlpool; beauty-barber salon, too. Very nice indeed. *Luxury.*

Lisboa Hotel (Avenida da Amizade; phone 377-666) is the only hotel in this book whose anything-but-friendly management refused to allow me to inspect even a solitary room, despite my presentation of credentials. There are, however, a thousand rooms—some in a recent wing, restaurants and bars, and a pair of casinos, which are the Lisboa's prime draw. *First Class.*

Presidente Hotel (Avenida da Amizade; phone 553-888) is a contemporary high rise sheltering 340 clean-lined rooms (doubles can be good-sized) with nice baths; a trio of restaurants (Occidental as well as Oriental), bar-lounge and disco-cum-entertainment. Quite central—not far, as a matter of fact, from the Lisboa Hotel, to which I prefer it. *First Class.*

Royal Hotel (Estrada da Vitora 2; phone 552-222) is at once modern and full-facility. By that I mean 350 nicely equipped rooms and baths, and a range of facilities including Chinese, Japanese, and European restaurants, coffee shop, bars, health club, and heated indoor pool. A link of the Japanese Dai-Ichi chain. *First Class.*

8

Macau to Eat and Drink

CUISINES OF PORTUGAL AND CHINA

Although it's not one of the great cuisines of Europe, Portuguese food can be very good indeed and in Macau it can turn up with unusual albeit tasty Chinese touches. If you've come from Hong Kong, as most Macau visitors do, you'll enjoy the difference in the restaurants of the two territories. Here are some specifics:

Afonso's (Hyatt Regency Macau Hotel, Estrada Almirante, Taipa Island; phone 321-1234)—yes, the "f" is correct, it's not an "l"—is the Hyatt's showplace restaurant. Go in the evening and the tables are candle-lit and a clutch of musicians strolls about, playing requests—even for "Melancholy Baby," if you like. The head chef has been brought out from Lisbon and prepares good things to eat. Roast Portuguese sausage, baked clams, or a choice of appetizers from a groaning buffet are among openers. *Caldo verde,* the Portuguese national soup, is good, and you may have *bacalhau,* or cod—Macau's favorite fish—half a dozen ways. Entrées based on seafood—the specialty—can be delicious; lobster under a mustard glaze and fried Macau sole and seafood stew among them. But there are steak or pork and veal chops if you prefer. Champagnes are French but most of the still wines are Portuguese—and good. Desserts? Off you go to the sweets table and choose as many as your plate will hold. *Luxury.*

A Lorcha (Rua do Almirante Sergio 289; phone 313-193) is neither very big nor very elegant. But it *is* very good. Fare is Portuguese—*caldo verde,* the soup specialty of the mother country, is a good starter, as might be shrimps or clams in a number of variations. Steaks are reliable—T-bone and veal steak among them, and a specialty is *feijoada,* based on pork and red beans, which I first came to know in Brazil. Cheerful service. *First Class.*

Amigo (Pousada Ritz, Rua da Boa Vista; phone 339-955) is interestingly international: U.S. prime tenderloin steaks, Scotch salmon, China Sea prawns, New Zealand lamb chops, Dutch veal. The indicated opener, at least if you're a snail buff like me, is *escargots Bourguignonne,* typically on the shell in French garlic sauce, with Caesar salad prepared at table a good alternative. *First Class/Luxury.*

Canton Tea House (Hyatt Regency Macau Hotel, Taipa Island; phone 321-1234): I was so pleased to find a restaurant with the original name of the Chinese city now called Guangzhou, that I stopped in with friends for a Cantonese dinner, which embraced such delicious dishes as sautéed beef in oyster sauce, stir-fried pork, braised duckling, and irresistible batter-fried shrimp. Very nice indeed. *First Class.*

Café da Barra (Pousada da São Tiago, Avenida da Republica; phone 378-111) offers Portuguese dishes with flair—in a venerable historic setting—roast sardines among openers, panfried filet of snapper with almonds, or sirloin steak as you prefer it, among entrées; the house's delicious *sonhos,* or fritters, among sweets. Welcoming ambience. *First Class.*

Dynasty (Mandarin Oriental Hotel, Avenida da Amizade; phone 567-888): You must order Dynasty's beggar's chicken—its version of a noted Hong Kong specialty—in advance, but it's worth doing. *Dim sum*—try the crab filet and ham wrapped with noodles—are tasty, too. And so are barbecues of duck, suckling pig, chicken, and pork, ideally presented in a combination platter. *First Class.*

Ease Garden (Rua Dr. P. J. Loboll; phone 562-328) may not sound Chinese, but is it ever—with excellent Cantonese specialties, and soothing tabs. *Moderate.*

Girassol Café (Mandarin Oriental Macau Hotel, Avenida da Amizade; phone 567-888): The hotel coffee shop—a U.S.-invented institution—has become popular in Asia. Girassol is a good example of the species, with an enormous menu in the American style albeit with local specialties, the range Thai prawn salad and crab bisque through panfried Macau sole, mixed grill, and baked pork chops, with American-style waffles, ice cream with flavors reminiscent of home, like marble fudge and almond praline, and—in preparation for this Yank grub—Scotch and soda or cocktails, including a really dry martini. *First Class.*

Fortaleza (Pousada da São Tiago, Avenida da Republica; phone 739-1216) is still another exemplary restaurant in the Pousada da São Tiago (see Café da Barra, above). Fortaleza, with the look of a colonial mansion of a much earlier period, is essentially Portuguese. Consider shredded cuttlefish salad to open, or if you're less adventuresome, seafood broth. The local variation on sole, Meunière or grilled, is good; and there are steaks and chops that you may want to order with their sauces on the side. If it's a hot day and a light lunch appeals, consider chef's or Caesar salads. *First Class.*

Jade (30 Avenida Almirante Ribeiro; phone 75126) might be just the ticket for a Chinese dinner based on specialties of Canton—the kind we know best in the U.S., employing pork, spareribs, shrimp, and chicken. *First Class.*

Lijinxuan (Pousada Ritz, Rua da Boa Vista; phone 339-955) is noted for Chinese seafood, braised abalone in oyster sauce, for example, or panfried prawn balls in lemon sauce. This is a good spot for pigeon—roasted or in half a dozen other ways. *Luxury.*

Maxim's-Henry's Galley (Avenida da Republica 4G; phone 76207) is beloved of locals for two prime reasons: jumbo spiced prawns and Macau-style African chicken. You'll have a good time. *First Class.*

Solmar (Rua da Praia Grande 11; phone 574-391) has made a reputation with delicious seafood, simply broiled if you prefer, or as the basis of one of the restaurant's own recipes. Like Maxim's-Henry's (above), its African chicken is tasty, too. *First Class.*

9

China's Top Three Cities to See and to Buy

BEIJING-SHANGHAI-GUANGZHOU (CANTON)

Hong Kong attracts for different reasons. Some of its visitors have stopped first in Japan and Korea and then journey south to Hong Kong. Others combine Hong Kong with other southeast Asian exploration, to, say, Thailand and perhaps the Philippines. Others of us enter Hong Kong *after* a trip through China. And then there is the substantial group—for whom this chapter is written—who visit Hong Kong *prior* to a Chinese interlude. Regardless of how or why you find yourself in Hong Kong, if you haven't been to China—or even if your visit was some years—or even a decade—back, when travel in that dynamic country was more adventure than pleasure, well, then, consider an excursion from Hong Kong.

My recent return to China after an eight-year absence was, to understate, an eye-opener. Aged hotels—in whose unadorned rooms singles in groups (then the only way to travel in China) shared with other singles—have been supplemented by modern, full-facility hostelries, many quite as luxurious as counterparts in Hong Kong—which is indeed going some.

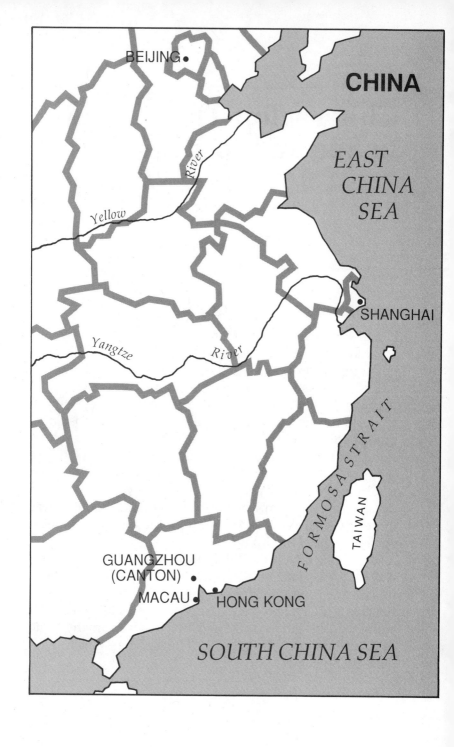

Currently, if you're on your own, you may have a room to yourself. Individuals or couples may now travel in China, not only groups. And, again, unlike the old days, you may reserve hotel rooms in advance as you would in any country. (Formerly, groups proceeding through China on a multistop tour learned the name and address of their hotel only upon arrival in each city, from the China Travel Service local guide for their group.)

There's no question but that the Tianamen Square shootout in 1989 that so shocked the world decimated tourist travel to China, ironically about the time of the opening of a network of new hostelries around the country. Nor is there any question but that today the Chinese are especially glad to see foreign faces. The recovery, with respect to tourism, from Tianamen Square is by no means complete. You still see proportionately more travelers in Hong Kong than in China. But people around the world recognize now, as indeed they have for centuries, that there is but one China, and that the world's most populous country—population exceeds a billion, despite an area only slightly larger than that of the U.S.—retains its distinctive, multifaceted culture (recorded history goes back four thousand years), languages, and cuisine, the lot immediately apparent to a visitor, an authoritarian Communist government notwithstanding.

Indeed, despite official Chinese resistance toward democracy, the welcome is warm and smiling, and English-language fluency is nothing less than extraordinary in major hotels, in important shops, and on tours, although, not yet at least, in restaurants outside of those in top hotels. (Not that you want to leave the beaten path in any big city and go off on your own even though it is indeed allowed; little English or other foreign languages are spoken by the population at large, and it's not difficult—believe me, I speak from experience—to get lost.)

From Hong Kong to China: You have several options. Many Hong Kong visitors sign up for brief, all-inclusive tours Hong Kong–China–Hong Kong, offered by a considerable clutch of Hong Kong–based operators. These journeys offer minuses as well as pluses. The latter is the help the tour operator is likely to provide in obtaining a Chinese visa for you in Hong Kong—something you can of course do by yourself as well. Additionally, the planning, guiding, restaurant (and meal) selection is all done for you, and if your trip is for more than a day, your hotel is selected by the tour operator, too.

Disadvantages? You go at a *very* fast pace, with the only free time (if the tour is more than a day) in the evening, postdinner. Additionally, even the shorter one-day tours to Guangzhou (ex-Canton) are invariably combined with a stop in a smaller, less interesting city, which, chances are, you would rather skip, adding the half day spent rushing through the smaller spot to big Guangzhou. Withal, these tours are godsends for in-a-hurry travelers who want to sample a bit of China while in Hong Kong and go either by train (it's not bad, and takes about three hours) *or* fly (a half hour) Hong Kong–Guangzhou–Hong Kong, staying at a hotel of your choice a night or two, with help from China Travel Service in sightseeing and other details, for you and your party—colleague, friend, spouse, or family.

I recommend allotting a full week for China, flying first from Hong Kong (via either Cathay Pacific or the Chinese national carrier, Air China/CAAC, to Beijing, staying, say, three nights; continuing then by air to Shanghai, for two nights, with the two final nights in Guangzhou (the major Chinese city closest to Hong Kong) before flying or taking the train back to Hong Kong.

An important prefatory note: If your plan is to depart Hong Kong by train for China, and if you have not arranged for your train ticket—or better yet, planned your China trip—

in advance, bear in mind that train tickets Hong Kong–China (Guangzhou is the first major stop) are *not* purchased in the Hong Kong Railway Station, but rather must be ordered *in advance*—as you would an air ticket—at one of the three Hong Kong offices of *China Travel Service (H.K.) Ltd.*—head office in CTS House (fourth floor), 78 Connaught Road, Central, Hong Kong; Central Branch at China Travel Building (second floor), 77 Queen's Road, Central, Hong Kong; and Kowloon Branch, Alpha House (first floor), 27 Nathan Road, Kowloon—the only one of the trio (unless hours change) open Sundays, customarily 9 A.M. to 1 P.M. and 2 P.M. to 5 P.M. Daily hours at all three offices are, customarily, Monday–Saturday 9 A.M. to 5 P.M. These offices reserve hotels in China; ask for their leaflet, *Hotel Reservation*, and give them as much lead time as you are able. Obtain as much information as you can before departing home from the *China National Tourist Office*, with branches at 60 East 42nd Street, New York, NY 10165, and 333 West Broadway, Glendale CA 91204; there are other branches in cities including Tokyo (13 Hamamatsucho, Minato-ku); London (4 Glentworth Street); Paris (51 Rue Ste.-Anne); Frankfurt (Escheheimner Anglage 28-D); and Sydney (55 Clarence Street). Remember, too, that visas are required for entry into China; you must leave your passport (with a photo), usually for a few days, at the Chinese Embassy, Consulate-General, or Consulate where you apply.

BEIJING

If it lacks the engaging flavor of once strongly European-influenced Shanghai, or the vitality of Guangzhou, Beijing, the national capital, compensates with size (it is packed with people) and significance. It is mostly flat, hardly beautiful, stretches for mile after boring mile. But there are pockets of beauty—no city, anywhere, has more superb Chinese art and artifacts on public display; the Great Wall of China is nearby, and there are top-of-the-line facilities for visitors (see Beijing to Stay), as well as irresistible shopping.

Palace Museum (a.k.a. Forbidden City, entered through the Meridien Gate at the center of the southerly arm of the moat that surrounds it, north of Sun Yat-sen Park) was for centuries (starting in the early fifteenth, when it was built) the home of emperors of the Ming and Qing dynasties— two dozen all told, in residence for a half a millennium. Figures for building the palace are staggering: there were a hundred thousand laborers in the work force, and an early-seventeenth-century rebuilding saw vast sums spent on the three great halls, each given a new look. The palace occupies an area exceeding seven hundred thousand square yards, with nine thousand rooms enclosed by a thirty-yard-high wall alongside its moat.

Most spectacular of the principal rooms is the Supreme Harmony Hall. Emperors reigned seated upon a gilded chair from the Golden Throne Hall, a veritable symphony in gold, with dragon-decorated gilded pillars its standouts. Today's Eastern Halls are Palace Museum galleries of porcelain, ceramics, bronzes, paintings, and other art, while the Western Halls are furnished as they were in premuseum days. Exhibits are of gold and ivory and porcelain and bronze and carved wood, the lot of them splendidly displayed. Give this museum time, ideally returning for a second visit.

Great Wall (northwest of Beijing) went up, originally, some twenty-five hundred years back, during what the Chinese call their Warring States era, but it was extended and fortified between the fourteenth and seventeenth centuries. Look it over at the point called *Bedaling* (with a museum dealing with the wall), which was a part of the Ming

Dynasty's northern defense system, cutting through rugged mountains near Juyong Pass, where it was as high as 25 feet and as wide as 21 feet, crossing five provinces and two autonomous regions. Allow a good half day.

Ming Tombs (not far east of the Great Wall, thirty miles from Beijing) is most definitely a plural. By that I mean there's not just one, there are a baker's dozen, one each for thirteen Ming Dynasty emperors, as old as the early fifteenth century when—and for a total of two hundred subsequent years—the tomb area was not open to the public. The tombs are at the end of a sculpture-flanked path and bridge, with one of the buildings, the Hall of Great Favor, identified as the largest ancient wood construction in China. Nearby Dingling Tomb is a dazzler, too; its opening as recently as the 1950s revealed some three thousand buried treasures, gold crowns among them.

Lugou Bridge (a.k.a. Marco Polo Bridge) is ten miles southwest of Beijing, built of stone, and notable for a series of eleven elegant arches that go back as far as the twelfth century; nearly five hundred stone lions embellish the bridge's low walls. The nearby city of Wanping is where, in 1937, Chinese troops first fired on invading Japanese forces, a prelude to the war that followed.

Summer Palace (northwest Beijing) is at once a vast green park edging also-vast Lake Kunming, and, as well, a network of historic pavilions, all romantically named, at least when they're translated into English, as for example, Jade Ripple Hall, Cloud Dispelling Hall, and Longevity Hall, the biggest. They're furnished in period, from the time of their construction, in most instances several centuries back.

Great Bell Temple (Third Ring Road, Beijing) takes the name of its immense bell cast in the early fifteenth century and weighing in at more than 46 tons. It can be heard many miles away. You're in luck here if you *really* like bells; there are 160 more. But they're smaller.

Grand View Garden (Garden Road) is actually a water-filled park—and of exceptional beauty, the mix towers and pavilions with forests and flowers, employing place-names—Peony Pavilion, Garden Lattice Nunnery, Autumn Freshness Studio, Bamboo Lodge, Paddy Sweet Cottage, Dripping Emerald Pavilion—that are among the most evocative in China.

Fragrant Hills Park (below Incense Burner Peak, northwest of town) is a forested mountain appealing enough to have been the site of palaces inhabited by a veritable mini-army of early emperors, and with temples for them to worship in, a number of which remain, including the temple taking the park's name (now in ruins). It is where the Central Committee of the Chinese Communist Party overnighted immediately preceding the formal founding of the People's Republic.

Western Hills' Eight Temples (Western Hills Park) include a pagoda with, legend says, one of the Buddha's teeth, and temples with Buddhist relics and sculpture, not to mention—in the case of some of the temples—fabulous views.

Yonghegong Lamasery (Yonghegong Street, in northeast Beijing) was the late-eighteenth-century home of one emperor (Yongsheng) and the birthplace of another (Quianlong), before it became a lamasery, whose five mural-filled main halls are chockablock with precious religious objects, fashioned from gold, silver, and sandal-wood.

Temple of Heaven (Temple of Heaven Park, south of the center) is actually a complex of structures in a tree-filled park of its own, and is as old as the fifteenth century—an era when it knew imperial worshipers. Core is the Hall of Prayer for Good Harvests, and if you must make a choice of buildings in the group, this is the one to inspect—with a hundred-foot-high conical tower constructed of wood but without nails, blue-tiled roofs, and a circular altar at which emperors participated in sacrificial ceremonies. And note the Echo Wall, so named because if you whisper while standing adjacent to it, your voice will be heard a considerable distance away.

Tianamen Square is the core of Beijing, and where, on October 1, 1949, Chairman Mao Ze-dong officially proclaimed the founding of the People's Republic of China. Its *Chairman Mao Memorial Hall* contains Mao's body in a crystal coffin. Rare is the group not taken to the hall; but of course you may go on your own. Also on this significant square are the *Great Hall of the People*, the city's biggest building and site of meetings of the National People's Congress; and, sharing a building, the *Museums of Chinese History and of the Chinese Revolution*, as well as the 124-foot-high *Monument to the People's Heroes*, a mix of white marble and granite.

Beijing Zoo (near Beijing Exhibition Center) is one of the world's best known, thanks in great part to its Chinese-origin pandas, including born-on-premises Yuanjin and Zhizi, born in the Shanghai Zoo and among the few pandas extant who have been bred in captivity. But there are other exclusive-to-China species, as well, including tufted deer and golden monkeys, Yangtze alligators and Tibetan donkeys. Feeding times, traditionally, have been 9 to 9:30 A.M. and 4 to 4:30 P.M. in winter; and 9 to 10 A.M. and 4:30 to 5 P.M. in summer. There's a restaurant, and it should go without saying, a souvenir shop at the Panda House.

Temple of the Azure Clouds (north of Fragrant Hills Park) is especially visitable for its 508 statues, or *arhats*, each with its own posture and facial expression, occupying a hall of its own in this thirteenth-century complex that also contains a pagoda as well as half a dozen courtyards, each on a separate level, edging a mountain.

Temple of the Reclining Buddha (in a parklike complex of its own almost immediately east of the Temple of the Azure Clouds (above) goes back to the pre-fourteenth-century Tang Dynasty, and reminds visitors who know Bangkok in Thailand of a similarly named temple in that city. Beijing's Reclining Buddha is cast of bronze, extends more than 15 feet in length and weighs in at 50 tons.

Beijing to Buy: Because it is the national capital, seat of the diplomatic corps, and the most important city for foreign visitors—few of whom miss visiting it—Beijing is China's principal shopping city. Give its stores some time, but not at the expense of retail outlets in Shanghai or Guangzhou, if they're on your own itinerary, remembering that you may well see things in other cities that did not turn up in Beijing. No. 1 shopper's destination is the *Beijing Friendship Store* (17 Jianguomen Wai Street), most celebrated of the republic's network of stores bearing the Friendship name, created for foreigners, and multifloor, department-store-style, with good-value, good-quality cashmere sweaters and other men's and women's clothing, brocaded silk robes and other silk goods, as well as objects of cloisonné, linen, and carved wood, carpets and household appliances in variety, tinned tea and packaged teabags, even Chinese spirits, wine, and medicines. Credit cards are accepted and many staff members are English-speaking. Also worth visiting are *China Arts and Crafts Trading Co.* (101 Fuxingmen Nei Street)—for gold and silver jewelry, jade, cloisonné, porcelain, embroidery, lacquerware, and traditional-style mahogany furniture (they ship); *Beijing Youth Friendship Store* (64 Nanxinhua Street)—for the clothes young Chinese wear, including Yank-style jeans and running shoes, and with electronic appliances, too; and *Beijing Jadeware Factory Store* (11 Guangming Road)—for jade in quantity and variety. Beijing makes much—too much, in my view—of its *Liulichang Street* shops, more of them than not without the antiques for which they are known (there are plenty of reproductions) and, as well, paintings and calligraphy, sculptures and assorted curios—the last mentioned inexpensive but frequently amusing. Most important of the main shopping thoroughfares is *Wangfujing Street*, in the center; allow yourself an hour or so to browse with the Beijingers, from *Western Style Clothes Store* at one end, to *Xinhua Bookstore*, at the other.

SHANGHAI

Not quite, but for all intents and purposes, nearly midpoint on the China Sea Coast, Shanghai is arguably the city-name, with Beijing, most associated abroad with China, in large part because it has figured as the setting for countless fictional accounts—Hollywood films, pulp mysteries, short stories, novels. Think China and you think Shanghai. It's the city that has known the most Western influence over the years, even extending to its skyline. Architecturally and in other respects as well, Westerners like Shanghai, and appreciate that unlike the two other of the Big Three cities (Beijing ex-Peking, and Guangzhou ex-Canton) it hasn't changed its name.

This is a big city—its immediate area has a population of more than a billion—yes, a billion—with some one hundred thousand shops and commercial establishments and ten thousand-plus factories. Shanghai's celebrated main street—the Bund—was developed in pre-World War II decades by European and other Western businesses; it boasts half a hundred skyscrapers, and along with Nanjing Road, it's fun to stroll, as a starter for visits to landmarks, including:

Jade Buddha Temple (Anyuan Road) is relatively modern— a 1918 refurbishing of a nineteenth-century original. Its magnets are a pair of white jade sculpted Buddha figures, seated each in a room of its own, and there is, additionally, a museum in the temple, with Buddha relics.

Shanghai Museum (Henan Road)—relatively recently and handsomely refurbished in toto, although still with no heat for winter visitors—is a world-class repository of Chinese art objects, a hundred thousand all told. Zero in on its paintings, bronzes, and ceramics especially—the bulk of considerable age and extraordinary beauty. Special.

Yu Yuan Garden (Nanshi) is a Ming Dynasty masterwork dating to the sixteenth century. Though not over-large—it covers two and a half acres—its striking design is what attracts—terraces and towers, bridges and rock formations along with some thirty no-two-alike scenic areas, stage set–like in the ingenuity of their design, fashioned of brick and carved wood, in architectural styles of the Qing and Ming dynasties.

Longhua Temple and Pagoda (Longhua Road, southwest of the core) date originally to the third century, but of course have been subjected to restorations and rebuildings. The pagoda stands out—octagonal and with seven brick and wood stories—while the temple, with extraordinary drum and bell towers, and no less than five principal halls, is the largest Buddhist house of prayer in Shanghai.

Shanghai Botanical Garden (Longwu Road) is perhaps most remembered for its miniature "garden within a garden"—plants in pots and miniature landscapes. But there are ten principal sections, the range azaleas and roses through bamboo and orchids. Eminently visitable.

Shanghai Zoo (Hongqiao Road) is especially worth knowing about should your China itinerary not include Beijing, whose zoo is world-famous for its pandas. Be advised that there are more of same in residence at Shanghai's zoo—among 350 species including such others as the Yangtse River alligator and the Northeast China tiger. Where you see a crowd of any size, it may well be that an animal is performing a trick—some do.

Sun Yat-sen's House (7 Xiangshan Road): The leader credited with having launched the Wuchung Uprising as a consequence of which the Qing Dynasty was overthrown and a Chinese Republic founded, Sun Yat-sen lived in this house between 1918 and 1924, not too many years after 1911—the year of the uprising—when he became provisional president of the new republic.

City God Temple Bazaar (a.k.a. Yu Tuan Bazaar, 119 Yuyuan Road) is a market named for the fifteenth-century temple that is its neighbor. You go principally, though, to take in the market's hundred shops where, rules insist, everything sold must be relatively small in size. That is indeed the case. Cafés, too.

Cruising the Huangpu River: If my time in a new city is relatively limited, I prefer remaining on dry land to see the sights close up, rather than detach myself on an excursion boat. However, this three-hour excursion is absorbing, especially after it leaves the core of the city for more distant parts. Refreshments are available on board.

Shanghai to Buy: Despite its enormous size, commercial eminence, and longtime relationship with the non-Asian world, Shanghai has relatively few stores catering to foreigners, compared at least to Beijing. *Shanghai Friendship Store* (694 Nanjing Road West) is the least cordial of the Friendship Stores in the three major cities, but it is very big and with good buys in lovely cashmere sweaters, robes of silk brocade, embroidery and linen, jade and cloisonné, lacquerware and bronze, scrolls and paintings, jewelry and carved bamboo. Credit cards are accepted albeit not graciously, and the staff, although with many English-speakers, is minimally cordial. *Shanghai Arts and Crafts Corporation* (1000 Yanan Road Central) has much of the kind of thing you will have seen at the Friendship Store—with good stocks of jade and cloisonné, porcelain and enamelware, traditional calligraphy and scroll-paintings. *Shangai No. 1 Department Store* (830 Nanjing Road East) is fun to explore—clothing and silk by the meter, kitchenware and appliances, Chinese watches and sewing machines, gold and silver jewelry, plastics and glassware. With a fifth-floor coffee bar. *Shanghai No. 1 Confectionery* (720 Nanjing Road East) is for as-you-travel nibbles—candy and cookies in particular. With lots of other food products, including Chinese wines and teas. *Shanghai Fashion Corporation* (690 Nanjing Road East) vends clothes and shoes for all the family—and reasonably. You may find some things you like. A number of the foregoing stores are on Nanjing Road, the main shopping street. This is a vibrant thoroughfare you want to explore with the loquacious Shanghainese, from its terminus on the Bund, west to the Friendship Store.

GUANGZHOU (FORMERLY CANTON)

Even in the case of cities we've never visited, we tend to react against changes of name. When we studied it in school it was Canton (at once easy to spell and to pronounce), but now we must come to terms with its new name, Guangzhou (say *guang-zhow*). This is the closest of the big southern cities to Hong Kong, and for that reason probably more visited from that point than any other. It fronts the South China Sea, is the seat of a world-class trade fair every spring and autumn (during fair periods hotel rooms can be difficult to obtain), and although it has fewer requisite places to visit than Beijing or Shanghai, it is big and busy and buoyant, so that if you've but, say twenty-four hours in China to add to a Hong Kong visit, consider an overnight journey to Guangzhou.

Chen Clan Academy (Zhongshangi Road) is an extraordinary complex—nearly twenty splendidly detailed buildings dating to the last decade of the nineteenth century. Principal function is to shelter the Guangdong Folk Arts Exhibition Hall, but Chen Clan is, first and foremost visitable for its architecture and design. As you wander through, take note of the detailed sculptures on the facades, the likewise elaborate embellishment of ceilings within; painted gates, lovely courtyards and roofs, the lot embracing brick-, stone-, and wood-carvings and cast-iron decorations on doors, gates, and moldings. This is one of Guangzhou's most exquisitely decorated buildings.

Liurong Temple and Pagoda (Zhongshan Road) goes all the way back (the history—not the building) to the sixth century, when the original temple was built alongside half a dozen banyan trees. To this day, Liurong is called Six Banyan Trees, as much as by its proper name.

Zhen Hai Tower (Yuexiu Park) is notable for two reasons: First is advanced age (at five stories it was for long after construction in 1380 the tallest building in town) and the second is its serving as seat of the *Guangzhou Museum*, municipal repository of historic objects related to Guangzhou's long history.

Guangzhou Temple (Renmin Road) is nothing if not old. Its history dates to the first century of the Christian era, and it has served as a private house, the anchor of a public garden, and finally a Buddhist temple. Its two towers are protected monuments.

Guangzhou Zoo (Middle Xianlie Road): Beijing's and Shanghai's are not the only zoos in China with pandas. This zoo has them, too, and such other rare animals as golden-haired monkeys, red-headed cranes, David's deer, and Chinese alligators.

South China Botanical Garden (near Longyandong, northeast of Guangzhou) is one of China's largest, with some four thousand species of plants. They're subdivided by type—shade plants, medicinal herbs, bamboo groves, and the like, so that you can look over a selection of species in each section.

Orchid Garden (near Liuhua Bridge) is accurately titled. There are no less than ten thousand pots of a hundred-plus species of orchids. If your visit is in autumn or spring, you're in luck: these are the seasons when they're in full bloom.

Yuexiu Park is Guangzhou's all-purpose park. By that I mean with a thirty-thousand-seat stadium and open-air theater, skating rink and art-exhibition hall, historic monuments and officials' memorials. Ask at your hotel about what is taking place during your stay.

Huaisheng Mosque (Zhongshan Road): Work started on this Moslem place of worship in the seventh century and it was completed in the tenth; it's one of the oldest mosques in China, still in use, and with a 110-foot minaret.

Guangzhou Foreign Trade Center (at Liuhua Bridge) is the site of the Chinese Export Commodities Fair, which takes place annually in the spring and autumn, with business execs from around the world joining Chinese colleagues as delegates.

Guangzhou to Buy: Guangzhou Friendship Store (379 Huan-shi Road East) is the visitor's prime source of Guangzhou specialties like embroidery and porcelain, as well as good-value, good-looking cashmere sweaters and other knit-wear and clothing, jewelry and appliances, inexpensive items like whimsically hand-painted wooden letter open-ers that make nice gifts for the gang at the office. There's a supermarket, too, with some of the packaged foodstuffs tempting. *Guangzhou Foreign Trade Central Market* (117 Liuhua Road) is visitable for its stocks of clothing for all the family, as well as appliances, curios, and a supermarket. You might find something you like at *Guangzhou General Gold and Silver Jewelry Shop* (199 Dade Road). Department stores are browsable—that called *Nanfang Dasha* (49 Yan-jiang Road West) and also—for toys, kids' togs, and wom-en's clothing—*Women and Children Department Store* (27 Xiajiu Road). And take a walk along busy Zhongshan Road, cutting through the city.

10

China to Stay and to Eat
Beijing, Shanghai, Guangzhou (Canton)

BEIJING

Beijing Hotel (East Chang Avenue; phone 513-7766) was the first hotel of my first trip to China—a decade back. So I'll always have a soft spot for it. That was during the period when you traveled in China only in groups. I was with a delegation of U.S. journalists invited to China by American Express, and in those days travelers going solo were doubled up in hotels with someone from their group; I was lucky that rather than drawing a stranger (which could and did happen on those tours) my roommate was a good friend and colleague, the noted travel writer/author Helmut Koenig. Although it opened as long ago as 1900 (it was for long the No. 1 hotel) and has of course been expanded, refurbished, and restyled over the years, its high point, for me at least, is its fabulous location—overlooking Tianamen Square to its right, and Wangfujing Avenue, a major downtown shopping street, to its left. The best thing about those of its 1,000 rooms I have seen are their terraces; insist on a room high up and with a good view; you won't forget the early morning vista from your terrace of what seems like thousands—and no doubt is—of citizens pedaling their bikes to work. Restaurants, with Chinese food the best bet. *Moderate/First Class.*

Beijing International Hotel (Jianguomennei; phone 512-5588) is among Beijing's newer hotels—it goes back a bit over a half decade and it's big: 1,049 rooms. Those I have inspected are good-sized and nicely appointed, with matching floral draperies and bedspreads, and good baths. There are suites, as well—nice, if the one I saw is typical. You've a choice of a dozen restaurants—Chinese, Italian, and a coffee shop among them; there's a beauty salon/barber shop, indoor pool, fitness center. And location is conveniently central. *Luxury.*

Beijing-Toronto Hotel (Jianguomennei; phone 500-2266) may sound Canadian, what with *Toronto* in the title, but it's operated by Nikko International, a Japanese chain. It's smaller than many of its giant counterparts in Japan (the Japanese adore hotels with enormous room counts); there are 668 rooms and suites. Those I have inspected are fitted out with tastefully understated textiles and marble-counter baths (some suites have two baths). The Chinese restaurant is the length of a city block, and there's a Western restaurant, along with a bar-lounge, indoor pool/fitness center, and business center. Fairly central. *Luxury.*

China World Hotel (Jianguomennai; phone 505-2266) is, as its name partially implies, a unit of an ultra-mod trade center called China World. Those of the 743 rooms and suites I have inspected are generous-sized; all have chaise lounges, pale-striped paper on their walls, and good baths—large, if those I've seen are typical. The lobby is a looker, and besides the bars you've a choice of Chinese, Japanese, and Western restaurants, and a coffee shop; and there's a well-equipped fitness center with a sixty-foot indoor pool, bowling, and squash. Fairly central. Affiliated with the Shangri-La International chain. *Luxury.*

Grand Hotel Beijing (East Chang Avenue; phone 513-7788) went up relatively recently as the Palace Tower—with its own entrance, reception, staff, and facilities—of the Beijing Hotel (above), and even more recently changed its name to Grand Hotel Beijing. Like the much bigger if inelegant Beijing Hotel proper, its ace in the hole is a superb situation, adjacent to Tianamen Square and with views from some accommodations (caveat: you must specify when booking) of the Forbidden City. There are 218 rooms and suites, and the Red Wall Café is highly recommended—generous and tasty buffet breakfasts through waitress-service dinner that is, conveniently, served very late. Member, Leading Hotels of the World. *First Class.*

Holiday Inn Downtown (Beilishilu; phone 832-2288) can be faulted only on its name. The "Downtown" of the title is a relatively recent commercial district a fair distance west of the Tianamen Square area, which is, of course, considered the heart of the city and the actual "downtown." There are just under 350 comfortable, modern rooms with reliable Holiday Inn baths, as well as also-reliable Western, Chinese, and Indian restaurants. Choice of bars, too, and a business center. *First Class.*

Holiday Inn Lido (Jichang Road): Well, compared to the Holiday Inn Lido, the so-called HI Downtown (above) is indeed downtown. The Lido unit is *way* away from the center, with a thousand-plus rooms (they can be small) with some for nonsmokers, extensive choice of restaurants, Western as well as Chinese, and an English-style pub among the bars; disco, indoor pool, and bowling alleys among other facilities. Convenient to the airport. *First Class.*

Jianguo Hotel (Jianguomennei; phone 595-2614): What I liked most about my inspection of the Jianguo was that it reminded me, from the moment of entry, that my visit occurred during the Year of the Goat; two live goats were relaxing in the lobby. There are some 500 okay rooms; Western, Chinese, and Japanese restaurants, a pair of bar-lounges. But you're quite a distance east of Tianamen Square. Only so-so. *Moderate.*

New Otani Chang Fu Gong Hotel (Jianguomennei; phone 512-5555): I am not a betting man but I would take heavy odds that should you book in here, you'll be the first on your block to have stayed at a hotel with a label as long as this one. Location is considerably west of Tianamen Square, but this 511-room house is agreeable enough, with rooms good-sized and comfortable (some are Japanese-style, with tatami matting), a nice view of the city from high-up accommodations, spiffy marble-floor *and* marble-walled lobby. Chinese and Western restaurants, fitness center/indoor pool, and business center. Japan's reliable New Otani chain is the operator. *Luxury.*

Kunlun Hotel (Xin Yuan Nan Lu; phone 500-3388) has, as its problem, at least as I see it, a location much more convenient to the airport than to the core of Beijing. This is a big, contemporary, good-looking house, with 28 stories and 853 clean-lined rooms and suites with super baths. I like the tapestry of the Kunlin Mountains, from which the hotel takes its name, that wraps around the lobby walls. There's a revolving Western restaurant on the roof; Japanese, seafood, and Chinese eateries as well; disco, fitness center and indoor pool. *Luxury.*

Palace Hotel (Wanfujing; phone 512-8899) is China's truly world-class hotel. I defy you to find a better hostelry—in any country, even Hong Kong, site of the great Peninsula Hotel, kingpin of the Peninsula Group, which operates the Palace. On scene only since 1990, the Palace—distinguished by contemporary exterior walls effectively teamed with a traditional Chinese pagoda-style roof—is heart-of-town, an easy walk to the Forbidden City, Tianamen Square, and principal shopping thoroughfares. You appreciate what its operation is all about when you consider that with but 578 rooms and suites (almost 60 of the latter are full suites, not including a score of junior suites) staff exceeds a thousand (of which a hundred-plus are expatriates, including a Dutch general manager, French executive chef, and British public relations director). Interiors are essentially European Traditional—and smart. The lobby is high-ceilinged, part glass-roofed, but not the excessively lofty atrium that has become a commonplace worldwide. Guest rooms are in pale tones, nicely appointed and with luxurious baths. The Palace Club is the premium-tab, extra-amenity section, with its own checkin-checkout, on-the-house laundry and cleaning, not to mention complimentary breakfast, cocktails, and canapés. The spa is anchored on a glass-roofed and -walled swimming pool adjacent to a fabulously equipped gym, sauna, aerobic studio, and massage salon. The Palace operates its own travel service: city and area tours you book through it are Palace-operated. There's an open-to-guests medical clinic, a tempting deli beloved of expatriate locals, billiard room, state-of-the-art business center that never closes, barber and beauty salons, trio of nightclubs—Rumours (a disco), Piccadilly (with dancing and entertainment), and Point After (singalong, Japan-origin *karaoke*). Restaurants? Each is an all-Beijing leader. There are two Chinese eateries—Fortune Garden (Cantonese) and Palace Restaurant (Szechuanese); the Japanese Inagiku (with its range *teppanyaki* through *sushi*); Champagne Room (so authentically French it could be in Paris); Roma (yes, so authentically Italian that it could be in the city whose name it takes); Bavaria Bierstube, with its own sausage-making master butcher (not every restaurant in Germany is *that* well equipped); and a coffee shop that specializes in buffets, breakfast through dinner, supplemented by an à la carte from which you may order what is arguably China's best hamburger. Member, Leading Hotels of the World. *Luxury.*

Shangri-La Beijing Hotel (Zizhuyuan Road; phone 241-2211) is for you, if you know—and have seen—Beijing, and are on business, ideally near the airport in the northwest part of the city, where the hotel is located. So long as you appreciate that you're a half hour's drive from the center of town, you can be happy in this handsome house, provided you've booked either a suite (they're lovely) or a superior category room—decent-sized and bigger than the small standard rooms generally used for groups. There are 786 rooms all told; extra-tab, extra-amenity Horizon Floor; health club including indoor pool and gym/fitness center-sauna; never-closed business center; and—worth a trip out from the city center—excellent restaurants, including Shang Palace (Cantonese), Brasserie (French), Peppino (Italian, and authentically so), coffee shop at once Oriental and Western, a bar with the look and feel of an English pub, and a disco. *Luxury.*

Ramada Asia Hotel (Xinzhong Xijjie; phone 500-7788) is among Beijing's newer hostelries, a sleek tower that looks as though it had more than 300 rooms (reason: 75 full-facility apartments for longer stays), an appealing variety of Asian and Western restaurants, bar-lounges, business and fitness centers. *Luxury.*

Tianping Lee Gardens Hotel (Jianguomennei; phone 515-8855) is operated by the same chain that runs the estimable Lee Gardens in Hong Kong, which you may know. Situation is in town albeit closer to the Friendship Store than to the core and Forbidden City. There are 430 well-equipped rooms, each with plenty of writing surface, for which praise be; Chinese and European restaurants and a coffee shop, pair of bars, business and fitness centers. *Luxury.*

Traders Hotel (Jianguomennei; phone 900-5106)—a near-neighbor of the China World Hotel—above—and in the same trade center both hotels share. This is a worth-knowing-about mid-category house. Those of the rooms—decorated in soft pastels—that I've inspected are good-sized and with good baths; there are some suites, too, and both Chinese and Western restaurants, as well as a bar-lounge. Shangri-La Hotels is the operator. *First Class.*

SHANGHAI

Galaxy Hotel (Zhongshan Road; phone 258-5052) is among Shanghai's newest—a striking curve of a tower, in white marble, with 840 attractive, contemporarily furnished rooms with bath, both Chinese and Occidental restaurants, bar-lounge, business center, bowling alley. Location is neither fish nor fowl; by that I mean you're not in the center nor are you at the airport, although the latter is closer to the Galaxy than the former. *First Class.*

Garden Hotel (Maoming Nan Lu; phone 433-1111): It's one thing to stroll the Bund, the riverfront thoroughfare that was the heart of the European quarter of pre-World War II Shanghai. It's another to actually live in a handsome, contemporary hotel the public spaces of which had been Shanghai's elegant French Club before the Second World War. Tokyo's ranking Hotel Okura—the Garden's operators—refurbished the club stem to stern, retaining those aspects of its original 1920s decor where appropriate, which with its appended tower (the hotel opened in 1989) makes it one of the best-looking hotels in Asia—high ceiling, colonnaded lobby—lounge, a quartet of restaurants—Chinese, European, Japanese (with *tempura* and *teppanyaki* among specialties), and a coffee shop at once charming and convenient. Guest rooms? There are 500—including a presidential suite in pale gray with an immense living room, formal dining room, pair of bedrooms and baths, study and guest bath—occupying the 34-story tower. Service? If you know the Okura in Tokyo, as I do, you will not be surprised to learn that it is white-glove, top-of-the-line. Member Leading Hotels of the World. *Luxury.*

Huagiao Hotel (Nanjing Road West; phone 276-2260) is an old-timer built by Europeans some sixty years back, in modified classical style with a graceful central clock tower. Situation is heart of Shanghai, on the main shopping street, where it is perpendicular with the riverfront thoroughfare called Bund. For some years the Huagiao had been designated an "Overseas Chinese" hotel—open only to visitors of Chinese origin from outside of China. Now, though, this house—alas, without the grandeur it must have known before World War II—welcomes guests regardless of where they're from. And its up-a-flight restaurant—delightfully old-fashioned in look, its tables dressed in immaculate white linen—is an excellent source of Chinese cuisine, especially nice on a day when you're roaming through town (although I must caution, service can be painfully slow—unusual in quick-as-a-wink China). There are 120 rooms with baths; size and decor varies. And not all that many of the staff are English-speaking. *Moderate.*

Jim Jiang Hotel (Mao Ming Road South; phone 582-582) is what America's Kennedy clan might call a compound. It's a clutch of buildings, with the senior among them the North Block, in modified Tudor style, dating to 1931, when it went up as a hotel for Shanghai's French community. Today's guests come from many lands (this was my first hotel in Shanghai, a decade back). Guest rooms are of varying sizes. There's a veritable network—eleven all told—of restaurants—Chinese of course, Japanese, Western—and bar-lounges, as well. *First Class.*   (Note also that the ever-so-contemporary *Jim Jiang Tower Hotel*, 161 Changle Road, phone 582-582 is within the Jim Jiang complex and has a half dozen restaurants, one revolving on the 42nd floor.) *First Class.*

Portman Hotel (Nanjing Xi Lu; phone 279-8888): Ask for a room on the north side of the Portman, as high up as you can go, and the view of the city will be memorable. This is a relatively recently opened hotel, near the Soviet-built Exhibition Hall, which, with its graceless albeit distinctive tower, is something of a Shanghai landmark, for better or for worse. At any rate, the Portman is good-looking, with a high-ceilinged and handsome lobby. Those of the 600 rooms I have inspected are agreeably soft-toned, in gray and mauve, and suites can be very nice, too. Executive Floors (42nd, 43rd, and 44th) are premium-tab with extra amenities including continental breakfast and complimentary cocktails. If you've a really fat budget, consider the 45th floor presidential suite. Lower down are Chinese, European, and Japanese restaurants, coffee shop, and bar-lounge. Not to mention indoor and outdoor pools, tennis, and both business and fitness centers. Operated by Shangri-La Hotels. *Luxury.*

Rainbow Hotel (Yanan Road; phone 275-3388) is a modern 661-room house, with accommodations—at least those I've inspected—attractive and well equipped; Chinese and Western restaurants, Japan-origin *karaoke* and other bars, big indoor pool, and business center. The lobby—pale blue-gray and white—is spectacular. And there's a pretty garden. *First Class/Luxury*.

Shanghai Hilton Hotel (Hua Shan Road; phone 550-000): Shanghai is proud of its Hilton—the first of that chain to open in China—as well it should be. The Hilton is a svelte 43-story tower, from which you may walk to the shops of Nanjing Road, and along that extensive thoroughfare all the way to the Bund. A smasher of a marble lobby leads into the Atrium Café, aptly titled and most spectacular of the hotel's restaurants, as satisfactory for lunch or dinner as for breakfast. The classy Teppan Grill is at once French and Japanese, with a teppanyaki counter for Japan's delicious grilled-before-you specialties. Still another restaurant, the Greenhouse, edges the indoor pool and serves Italian fare. Chinese cuisine? You take your choice of three restaurants—Sui Yuan for Cantonese specialties; Sichuan Court for the spicy food of Szechuan, of which we're so fond in New York, where I live; and Shanghai Express, for Shanghainese fare, most underappreciated of the major Chinese regional cuisines. Sichuan Court shares the 39th floor with the Penthouse, a bar-lounge that specializes in drinks accompanied by panoramas, and is super at sunset. There are 775 guest rooms with all the comforts of Hilton International, minibar and in-house movies through to writing tables with plenty of surface, and tasteful decor in tones of beige and gold. Executive floors are premium-tab and extra-amenity, with continental breakfast, snacks the day long, and cocktails with canapés all on the house. The business center is open round the clock, so that you can be in touch with head offices, no matter the time of day or evening. And the fitness center, adjacent to the pool, includes a sauna and massage room, as well as tennis and squash courts. Bravo, Hilton International! *Luxury*.

Shanghai Mansions Hotel (Suzhou Road; phone 324-6260) predates World War II (it had another name then) and although it has known bouts of refurbishing in recent decades, is not a spot you're going to write home about. Rooms are of varying sizes and decor styles. There's a so-so Chinese restaurant, and not many of the staff speak English. *Moderate.*

Westin Tai Ping Yang Hotel (Zin Yi Nan Lu; phone 275-8888): You'll be forgiven if you refer to this one simply as the Westin. This is a honey of a hotel that lacks only a central situation; it's out near the airport, and might be convenient if you've time for a brief Shanghai interlude between flights. (The concierge can arrange tours as brief as half a day.) This is a good-looking, up-to-the-minute, 578-room house (marble baths are exceptional) of the caliber that has given Westin a well-deserved reputation. Public spaces—lobby, Chinese and Japanese restaurants, Western-accented Cafe Bristol, and the oft-lively bar-lounge—appeal. There's an extra-tab, extra-amenity Executive Floors section with breakfast and cocktails included in the rate; business and fitness centers; and a tempting deli—for the homesick. *Luxury.*

GUANGZHOU

Bai Yun Hotel (Huanshi Dong Road; phone 333-998) is an ever-so-contemporary 34-story, 700-room high rise that's one of the tallest buildings in Guangzhou. It is not, however, central. Still, if you don't mind being away from the heart of town, near one of the city's big parks, you will be content enough. Both Chinese and Western restaurants, bar, coffee shop, even a billiard room. *First Class.*

China Hotel (Liu Hua Lu; phone 666-8888) is one of the city's leaders, with 1,200 rooms—those I have seen are

tasteful and with good baths—and more restaurants—
Chinese and Western—than you'll have time to sample, I
venture, unless your stay is a long one. Other facilities,
too—health club with gym and sauna, outdoor pool, disco,
even a nine-lane bowling alley. *First Class.*

Dong Fang Hotel (Liu Hua Road; phone 669-900): The
name sounds like the title of a corny movie, but the Dong
Fang is an agreeable hotel with restaurants, bar, convention facilities, outdoor pool, tennis, squash, and business
center. Away from the center. *First Class.*

Garden Hotel (368 Huanshi Dong Lu: phone 338-9890) is,
to understate, a biggie, with 1,100 rooms, and half a dozen
restaurants, evenly distributed between Chinese and Western, outdoor pool, gym, disco, and a business center. Operated by the people who run the Lee Gardens, which you
may know in Hong Kong. Unless something larger comes
along, this is the biggest hotel in town. *Luxury.*

Holiday Inn City Center (28 Guangming Lu; phone 766-
9999) is architecturally striking from without, and doesn't
disappoint within, what with 431 pleasant rooms (including 40 suites), a number of restaurants, both Chinese and
Western, bar-lounge, pool, disco, health club, and business center. *Pas*, as the French say, *mal. First Class.*

Plaza Hotel (383 Jiang Nan Da Road Central; phone 418-
8888); If you go back some years in Guangzhou, you may
remember the Plaza as the Novotel. It's a 450-room double
tower, with Western and Chinese restaurants and coffee
shop, bar-lounge, a swimming pool, and a gym. This is a
nice hotel but it's not central. *First Class.*

White Swan Hotel (Shamian Island; phone 886-968) is a
case of saving best for last. The White Swan, with its is-

land location, has the Pearl River on one side, gardens on the other. To note that this 886-room-and-suite hotel is well equipped is to understate. Spaces are big, baths are marble-accented, the presidential suite is one of the most sumptuous in China, and restaurants are diverse, the range a coffee shop and tea lounge through the Jade River for Cantonese fare; Silk Road—an absolute Guangzhou requisite for European fare; and Hirata, a Japanese spot. The health club is a standout; there are a pair of swimming pools, both squash and tennis courts (eight of the latter, if you please), golf driving range, jogging track, wee-hours disco, even an Elizabeth Arden beauty salon. This is one of China's best-equipped hotels. Member, Leading Hotels of the World. *Luxury.*

A note about non-hotel restaurants: Restaurants outside of hotels specializing in foreign guests—the better ones, especially, like those above, in this chapter—can impress with size (some have a dozen-plus dining rooms feeding in excess of a thousand customers per meal) and on ambience; there's no better way to watch China at its leisure. But there are drawbacks. Most important is language; very few staffers in very few restaurants speak English or other foreign languages. And second is housekeeping. By that I mean table linen is not changed with the arrival of each new party of diners, napkins are not always available—that kind of thing. And at crowded periods, service can be painfully slow. If you are traveling with a guided group, you simply follow the leader when out-of-hotel restaurants are selected, and you eat what is served you, like it or not. (Upon occasion, you will not, but it will be edible.) If you are with a Chinese-speaking person, you might want to try the *Quanjude Roast Duck Restaurant* (13 Shuaifuyuan Street, off Wangfujing Street, Beijing)—where the specialty is Peking (or Beijing) duck, as has been the case since the original restaurant opened in 1864, and where you will be among as many as 3,000 diners served in forty-one rooms on seven floors; *Sichuan Fandian* (51 Rongxian Hutong West, Beijing)—for the hot and spicy cuisine of Szechuan; *Beijing Maxim's* (2 Chongwenmenxi Street, Beijing) for French-style fare that is —to understate—by no means always successful; *Shanghai Laofandian* (242 Fuyou Road, Shanghai)—dating to the 1860s, with eight-treasure duck, braised fish, and fried spareribs prime specialties; *Yangzhou Restaurant* (308 Nanjingdong Road, Shanghai) for its chicken, shrimp, and fish dishes; *Hu Xin Ting* (Yu Yuan Gardens, Shanghai), a 180-year-old tea room—utterly captivating to look upon—occupying two floors, with the second-floor space the most outrageously expensive I have encountered in China for tea—individual clay pots in which it's served (each person must order his or her own pot) notwithstanding; *Guangzhou Restaurant* (2 Wenchangnan Road, Guangzhou)—for suckling pig, roast goose, and—if you're up to it, during the season, in autumn—Guangzhou-style snake; and *Datong Restaurant* (63 Yanjiangxi Road, Guangzhou)—for its crisp-skin chicken and its shrimp dumplings.

Please let me repeat: non-hotel restaurants can be worth a try if you're in the company of a Chinese-speaking person. Otherwise, concentrate on the invariably commendable hotel restaurants—Western as well as Chinese—that I call to your attention on earlier pages of this chapter. Standards and staffs can change, but by and large, restaurants in hotels for foreigners are attractive, spotless, professionally staffed, English-speaking—and delicious.

Acknowledgments

Though I have been a fairly regular—and invariably enthusiastic—visitor to Hong Kong over a sustained period, on-scene research for an all-encompassing book such as *Hong Kong at Its Best* required substantial settling-in. I have been fortunate indeed with help, support and cooperation received in the course of exploring Hong Kong in depth for this book, and I want to express special appreciation to a number of friends and colleagues.

Cynthia L. Fontayne, whom I started working with in New York some years back, when she represented Swissair to the American press, has deserted the Big Apple in favor of the West Coast, where she represents Hong Kong-based Cathay Pacific Airways. She has been enthusiastic about this book from the outset, as indeed has Mary Testa Bakht, the crackerjack New York-based public relations manager of the Hong Kong Tourist Association for the United States, and Torre Ossmo, HKTA's president for the United States, based in Chicago. Mary Bakht and her associate, Edith Wei—both with extraordinary Hong Kong expertise—have been ready with answers whenever I needed them. Yanjun Zhou, former director of the China National Tourist Office in New York, and Bo Wu, assistant director, have been cooperative with respect to my research in China for the chapter on that country. And Brian E. Williams, general manager of the Mandarin Oriental Macao, was especially helpful in Macao.

Max Drechsler, research editor for my books, and like me a longtime admirer of Hong Kong, was of immeasurable assistance in the course of the final—and extensive—research trip, and I am as always grateful for the support of my agent—still another Hong Kong buff—Anita Diamant. Michael Ross, editorial director of Passport Books, and my editor, knows and likes Hong Kong, too; he has been skilled and sympathetic, as always; this is the thirteenth book (not including a substantial number of revised editions!) on which we have worked together.

I want also to thank, alphabetically, the following friends and colleagues with whom I have worked in the United States and in Hong Kong, China and Macau, in the course of researching *Hong Kong at Its Best*, for personal kindness and professional cooperation: Judi Arundel, Thomas Axmacher, G. C. Balenieri, David Bell, Felix Max Bieger, Diego Bozzolan, Han C. W. Brouwers, Bob Burrichter, Jerome Chan, Danny Chan, Patsy Chan, Y. M. Chan, Eric C. I. Chang, William Chen, Fu Chuanwen, Jessica Cheung, Sherman Cheung, Zion Chung.

Also Colin P. Clark, Jerry W. Davidson, Zhang Zong Dao, Tan An Di, Karen Weiner Escalera, June Farrell, Eileen and Fred Ferretti, Miki Magome Funai, Dorothy Furman, Lynn Grebstad, Giovanni Greggio, Sian Griffiths, Anna Guerreiro, Linda C. Gwinn, May Ho.

Also Selina Hung, Li Zhen Jiang, Mario Goretti Kam, André Kretschmann, Hubert Kuchar, Lydia Kung, Eva Kwan, Gisèle Kwan, Joanne Lao, May Law, Jennie Lee, Jessica Lee, Harry Huang Yan Lei, Chang Shi Ling, Susanna Wong Lok, Karisa Yuen-Ha Lui.

Also Denis G. Martinet, Quinnie Ng-Quinn, Rolina Pang, Daniel Pellegrinelli, Robert A. Piccus, Carol Poister,

Wang Rong Qiong, Tommaso Ragusa, Darrio Regazzoni, Deng Bu Rong, Sig T. San Jose, Heinz J. Schwander.

Also Donna Simmons, Samuel Sing, James A. Smith, Gillian Stevens, Gerhard Stutz, Claudia Swain, Zhang Tian, Patrick Tong, Allan Tsang, Simon Tse, Robert W. Van der Ham, Daniel Vong, David Wan, Stephen W. H. Wan.

Also Julie Wilson, Georgina Wong, Marina Wong, Stephen Wong, Ye Xinru, Simon Yeung, Zhai Qian Yi, Cui Yingming, Zhou Yonghua, Bennette Yung, Rena Zhao, and Kerry Green Zobor.

R. S. K.

Index

INDEX

ABOUT THE AUTHOR

Robert S. Kane's initial writing stint came about when, as an Eagle Scout, he was editor of the [Boy Scout] *Troop Two Bugle* in his native Albany, New York. After graduation from Syracuse University's noted journalism school, he did graduate work at England's Southampton University, first making notes as he explored in the course of class field trips through the Hampshire countryside. Back in the U.S., he worked, successively, for the *Great Bend* (Kansas) *Daily Tribune, Staten Island Advance, New York Herald Tribune,* and *New York World-Telegram & Sun* before becoming travel editor of, first, *Playbill,* and later *Cue* and *50 Plus.* His byline has appeared in such leading magazines as *Travel & Leisure, Vogue, House & Garden, Atlantic, Harper's Bazaar, Family Circle, New York, Saturday Review,* and *Modern Bride;* and such newspapers as the *Newark Star-Ledger, New York Post, New York Daily News, New York Times, Los Angeles Times, Chicago Sun-Times, Boston Globe, San Diego Union, Dallas Morning News, San Francisco Examiner,* and *Toronto Globe & Mail.* And he guests frequently, with the subject travel, on TV and radio talk shows.

Africa A to Z, the first U.S.-published guide to largely independent, post-World War II Africa, was the progenitor of his acclaimed 14-book *A to Z* series, other pioneering volumes of which were *Eastern Europe A to Z,* the first guide to the USSR and the Soviet Bloc countries as seen through the eyes of a candid American author, and *Canada A to Z,* the first modern-day, province-by-province guide to the world's second-largest country. His current 13-volume *World at Its Best* series includes two titles *(Britain at Its Best* and *France at Its Best),* tapped by a pair of major book clubs, and a third *(Germany at Its Best)* that's a prize-winner.

Kane, the only American authoring an entire multivolume travel series, has the distinction of having served as president of both the Society of American Travel Writers and the New York Travel Writers' Association, and is a member, as well, of the National Press Club (Washington), P.E.N., Authors Guild, Society of Professional Journalists/Sigma Delta Chi, and American Society of Journalists and Authors. He makes his home on the Upper East Side of Manhattan.